Let's
Cook
FOR OUR DOG

Let's
Cook
FOR OUR DOG

Written and Illustrated
by
Edmund R. Dorosz, B.S.A., D.V.M.

R.I.P. 2000

Let's Cook
FOR OUR DOG

First Edition September 1993

Canadian Cataloguing in Publication Data

Dorosz, Edmund R., 1944-
Let's cook for our dog

Includes index.
ISBN 0-9696884-0-7
1. Dogs--Food--Recipes. 2. Dogs--Nutrition.
I. Title.
SF427.4.D67 1993   636.7'085   C93-091716-2

Published and distributed by
Our Pet's Inc.
P.O. Box 2094
Fort Macleod, Alberta, Canada
TOL OZO

Printed and bound in Canada by D.W. Friesen and Sons

CONTENTS

ACKNOWLEDGMENTS

I would like to thank my wife Sandra for her support and my children Sean and Sarah for putting up with my dream of this kind of book for five years. I have to mention our black lab "Turk" for being such a willing tester for all of my recipes. Thanks as well are extended to Rhonda Henke of Major Graphics, Precision Colour Imaging Ltd., Jim Beckel of Friesen Printers and David Poulsen, author and English Instructor for their professional assistance.

I acknowledge my late parents: E.C. Dorosz for always praising my art productions and encouraging me to higher education and Stephanie Dorosz for her artistic genes, love of cooking and recipe collection.

Lastly, I would like to acknowledge my students and veterinary patients who inspired my interest in practical nutrition, and the owners of these animals for their many questions.

NOTE TO READERS

This book is an educational and informative guide for feeding our dog. The recipes have all been tested and no harm can be encountered if the directions are followed. One single recipe should not be the sole source of food over any length of time. Variety is best.

The Goals of this book are:

- To present as simply as possible an understanding of our pet's basic nutritional requirements for an active and healthy life.

- To evaluate commercial dog foods so that informed shopping decisions can be made.

- To provide recipes prepared from fresh ingredients found in our kitchens.

Since we feed our pets every day and every individual pet is different, it is up to us to determine if our pet is being adequately looked after. There is an old saying that "Nutrition is in the eye of the Feeder". The feeder must observe the pet and make adjustments to the diet based on those observations.

There are five parts to this book: Nutrition and Nutrients, Commercially Prepared Dog Food, Getting Started, Recipes and Nutritional Related Problems.

It has been my goal to simplify dog nutrition so that we can all understand what we are doing when we feed our dog. We can apply this basic knowledge to the art of cooking for our dog. However, when we simplify, many details are eliminated and exactness can suffer.

I have deliberately stayed away from too many Do's and Don't's, Must's or Must Not's in this book. I have been in this business long enough to develop gray hair by having someone prove me wrong when I have made a rigid statement. There are many examples in everyday life that were gospel yesterday but not today. We've heard: no bones, no table scraps, no vitamins or mineral supplements are necessary; dogs don't need vitamin C and the list goes on. Many times in my professional career as a practicing veterinarian, I have been proven wrong when giving strict advice for animal nutrition and health.

I believe that there are those of us in advisory professions, who get in a rut. We tend to give yes-no answers to questions when maybe the solutions are more gray than black or white.

When dealing with animal nutrition and health, many factors are involved as each animal and situation is unique. Feeding and animal care is an art as well as a science. Some of us are better at the art than others. The final picture is the health and well being of our dog.

I have attempted to explain as simply as possible with words and pictures many aspects of nutrition and feeding so that we can make knowledgeable decisions on what is best for our pet. We live with our pet everyday and are the ones who must make these decisions. Our dog will tell us what is best for him or her and we must be able to respond to his or her needs.

Nutrition is a big part of health, but if a medical problem is suspected we should seek good veterinary medical advice.

Good luck, and remember to watch and listen to our dog as he or she will tell us what is right for them. It is up to us to be smart enough to understand what our dog is telling us.

INTRODUCTION

Cooking for Our Pets

We can do "our own thing,"
with a little knowledge,
a little extra planning, and
a little preparation,
we can offer our pets meals that are:
cheaper,
free of additives and preservatives
as fresh,
as nutritious,
as tasty,
and with as much variety,
as the meals we serve our family.

"Cooking is an Art, a part of the cultural pattern of society"
Gladys C. Peckham.

*"The feeding and care of your pet is a pleasant responsibility.
Know that you could be making one of your family happy
today."*
Bernard Tonken, DVM.

*"Keeping your cat and dog friends happy through a good diet
is not difficult and you will be rewarded many times over."*
Joan Harper.

A cookbook for dogs? Why not? There are thousands of cookbooks for people but I could find very few for our pets. Why not research and write a book for our pets with recipes especially for the dog?

In North America and Europe we spend billions of dollars every year on pet foods that are prepared, processed, and packaged great distances from where they will be eventually eaten. What happened to feeding fresh people food to pets, and where are the recipes for preparing people food for our pets?

Prepared commercial pet food is wonderful stuff: handy, simple, and available. However, it is not perfect. If we are to feed our dog properly, a basic knowledge of canine nutrition and a little effort are required.

Before we get started we should review our pet's basic nutritional requirements and understand what we are doing when we feed our dog. We must also appreciate the dog's digestive system and how it is different from that of other animals and our own. As with any topic, knowledge is our greatest tool.

Commercially prepared dog foods are available to us today so we should take full advantage of them, know what we are buying, and understand the pitfalls.

The recipes in this book were developed and tested with appreciation of the differences between us: man and dog. The recipes can be prepared with ingredients that we are familiar with and can be modified if we care to. Remember that cooking is an art as well as a science. No single diet or recipe should be the sole source of food over any length of time. "Variety is the spice of life" for all of us. Variety also helps to insure that all nutrients are present.

We must always remember that dogs, like people, are individuals and what is good for one may not be good for another. Recipes and commercial dog foods are developed for the average individual and we must always ask, "What is average?" We also assume that the dog we are feeding is normal and healthy. If we have an individual that may have some abnormality, perhaps he or she should be under veterinary supervision.

This is a book for the dog, with sections on nutrition and nutrients, commercial dog foods, recipes that we can prepare and nutritional related problems. I hope that you have as much enjoyment feeding your dog as I had in writing and illustrating this book.

PART ONE Nutrition and Nutrients

"Dietary management is the lifelong daily control of nutrient intake to meet the changing unique requirements of both healthy and diseased pets, in order to maximize the quality and length of life."
Hills, *Small Animal Nutrition.*

Nutrition does not have to be difficult to understand and yet, when we look around at the human species, we may conclude that very few of us understand even the basics. We are going to discuss the basics of nutrition and how they apply to the dog, and then with this knowledge we will be able to feed our pet.

What is nutrition? Nutrition is the consumption of food of sufficient quality and quantity that will permit an animal to reach and maintain a body condition of which it is genetically capable within its given environment. Another way to define nutrition would be the digestion and processing of foods into substances that the dog's body can use, and nutrients as the substances that the dog requires for living. In other words, foods: how, why, and what they do for the dog's body.

When animals are provided with the proper nutrients in adequate amounts, they will flourish to their inherited potential.

In this section we will further define nutrition, discuss digestion and absorption, outline the basic nutrients, and then specify how we can provide foods with these nutrients thus enabling our pets to achieve good health.

For us to provide our pet with an adequate diet we must have a basic understanding of the dog's nutritional requirements and the food sources of these requirements. As owners of the today's dog, we are in total control of what and how much it will eat, as compared to a dog in the wild who can wander and pick its own food. Since our dog totally depends upon us and has no choice, we should have some understanding of nutrition.

In other words:
- what are the requirements for activity, growth, and play?
- what foods contain these requirements? and
- how do we provide these foods in adequate amounts?

Perhaps we have not really thought about it in this manner. If the food that we feed our pet does not meet these requirements, trouble is just over the horizon.

For a dog's food to fulfill these requirements the food must:
- be palatable,
- supply enough energy for the particular daily energy needs
- have the proper nutrients in the correct amounts and balance for adequate growth and repair of tissues
- be digestible and utilized by the dog.

With these four "must's" we feed our pet everyday, keeping him in a state of good health.

When is our pet healthy? We, as the sole providers of food and shelter, have taken on the responsibility of maintaining this individual in a state of good health. Therefore we must always be on the look-out for the signs of good health.

Some signs of good health and nutrition are:
a good appetite,
proper weight,
alertness,
glossy haircoat,
regular urination and defecation,
and vigor.

For us to formulate recipes for our dogs, we must have some basic understanding of their make-up. Dogs, Canis familiaris (Ka-nes fe-'mil-yer-es) are carnivores, living on the flesh of other animals just as they have done for millions of years. Because animal flesh was the diet for many years, their digestive systems are especially suited for this. There are other basic differences too. For example, their teeth are sharper, intestines shorter, and livers larger. Eating habits were also different. Dogs eat occasional big meals containing primarily protein and fat, and they tend to gorge themselves. In between these big meals they rest and nibble. Cows and horses, on the other hand, are herbivores or vegetarians, spend a lot of time eating small amounts often. Herbivores also have large digestive systems and must get the help of microorganisms such as bacteria to digest plant material.

The dog of prehistoric time did not just eat the flesh of its prey but the complete carcass, including hair, bones, organs and the contents of the stomach and intestines. The wild cousins of the domestic dog have these same eating habits today. By consuming everything, our dog's ancestors had access to vegetables, cereals, fruits and berries when they ate these contents. This is how they obtained many of their required nutrients such as some vitamins and minerals that may not be present in flesh alone. Often the prey of these dogs was a herbivore that ate strictly plant matter, and its stomach would be filled with partly digested plant material.

We have to remember this when we feed our dog cereals and vegetables. If we partially cook or grind this type of food, the dog is better able to digest it, consequently getting the most benefit with the least problems.

Dogs also have the ability to vomit quite readily, again from necessity. Wild dogs often had to devour their food in a hurry because they were competing with others at the same meal and if they didn't hurry they may not have got anything to eat. By ripping, tearing and then swallowing in a hurry with very little chewing, large pieces of tough gristle and fragments of bones would be swallowed. Vomiting then would be an asset as this material could be brought back up at a quieter moment away from the crowd and be either chewed and reswallowed or disregarded. Having this natural ability to vomit prevented a lot of problems, so we should not become too upset if our dog occasionally vomits. If, however, our dog should persistently vomit, something could be wrong and a visit to a veterinarian may be called for.

Vomiting is also a way for the wild dog's parents to feed their young. The adults would eat whatever they had hunted and then deliver this back in their stomachs to provide partially digested food for the young back at the den.

The eating habits of the dog for millions of years did not change much. As a carnivore roaming freely, he ate what he could catch as a hunter. Some days were good and others were not. With domestication and confinement, our modern dog does not have to hunt for his next meal. However, he cannot pick and choose. He must eat what we give him. The dog has become totally dependent upon us. Not that long ago, the domesticated dog was fed table scraps and whatever he could pick up from his wanderings about the neighborhood. In the last seventy-five years, the commercial processed dog food industry has evolved, which offers the modern dog owner a wide variety of totally prepared food. The dog of today is totally dependent upon us for his diet and well being.

Modern science has discovered and identified many nutrients. We know a lot about nutrition but still have a lot to learn. It seems that every day we hear something about an unknown nutrient or how we should or should not eat a known one. We must always keep this in mind when feeding our dog today. Maybe we ought to be more flexible in what we give our dog to eat, so that he is not missing something that modern science has not yet discovered. The dog's body is a wonderful, complex organism with great abilities to adapt. Some individuals may not adapt. With the many changes to the dog's environment, we are now seeing " diseases of domestication and confinement." We are seeing nutritional and behavioral problems in our confined dogs. Some feel that the dog should be fed a variety of foods, including fresh food, as opposed to a constant diet of processed food; then his diet will be more like it was before we changed his environment.

Carol Barfield, petfood activist, *"My ideal petfood includes four elementary concepts; variety, moderation, suitable for human consumption, and fresh food daily."*

Modern veterinary training, in my opinion, is quite limited in the field of nutrition and tends to place greater emphasis on pharmacology or drug therapy. Thank goodness we have many life saving pharmaceuticals available today. I believe, however, that many diseases and problems with our dogs have poor nutrition as an underlying cause. What our dog eats will determine how he will grow and if he will live a happy and healthy life.

We are in the best position to determine if our dog is healthy because we see our pet every day. If we see signs such as poor appetite, poor hair coat, or lack of vigor, inadequate nutrition may be the cause. It is our duty to beware of these signs of poor nutrition and make corrections.

The basic food requirements for the dog can be broken down into six main areas. In order for the dog to function these must be present in varying proportions depending upon the individual's particular needs.

The six main groups of nutrients are:

- Water
- Carbohydrates
- Proteins
- Fats
- Vitamins, and
- Minerals.

Foods have some or all of these nutrients in them, and dogs need these nutrients in varying amounts on a regular basis. Nutrient requirements will vary with such things as age, breed, activity, and temperament. Each dog is an individual with specific requirements; therefore, the amounts will differ. Differences may not be that great between two dogs, but over time may become obvious. For example, if we fed two dogs of different size the same diet everyday, one may become overweight, and the other may lose weight. From this simple example we can see the obvious. One dog was getting too much to eat and the other not enough for their individual requirements.

When all of the nutrients are provided in the correct proportions we say that the diet is "balanced."

Refer to the picture on page 19 and see how the dog is balanced on the teeter-totter with the six nutrients: water, carbohydrate, protein, fat, vitamins and minerals.

Balanced Requirements

Water
  Carbohydrates
    Protein
      Fat

Vitamins
Minerals

Dog
fed for
one week

In the picture the nutrients are placed on the teeter-totter in order of importance, with water being out on the end, then carbohydrates on to vitamins and minerals nearer the center. This is not to say that vitamins and minerals are less important, but if we should take water away from the dog he will suffer very quickly. However, it may take months for a shortage of a vitamin or mineral to show a noticeable difference in the dog.

The size of the containers of the various nutrients on the teeter-totter roughly illustrate the amounts of each that would maintain an adult dog with normal activity. If we could fill the water container with water, the carbohydrate container with pure carbohydrate, the protein container with pure protein, the fat container with pure fat, and provide the vitamins and minerals accordingly, this dog would be fed for a week. Unfortunately, it is not that simple; however, this is a good model to remember.

How are things different? First, the size of the containers will vary with the dog on the other end. If the dog is a growing puppy, for example, the protein container would have to be larger because a growing puppy requires more protein for the growth of muscles and other tissues. Vitamins and minerals would also have to be increased as the puppy would need more for bone growth. If the dog on the other end of the teeter-totter was a working dog such as a sled dog, the fat container would be larger, as this type of individual requires greater amounts of highly concentrated energy. We would make the carbohydrate and fat containers smaller if the dog was neutered or overweight because we would want to lower the energy amounts fed for this dog to lose weight.

Another problem with this model is that foods, with few exceptions, are really mixtures of nutrients. For example, a piece of meat contains water, protein, fat, and some vitamins and minerals. A slice of bread is mostly carbohydrate with some proteins, vitamins and minerals. Few foods contain only one nutrient.

Because foods are mixtures of nutrients, the dog's digestive system must break down the foods eaten into the various groups. Once the foods are separated into water, carbohydrate, protein, fat, vitamins and minerals, the process continues so that the nutrients will become acceptable for his use. The other consideration when dealing with foods and the different amounts of nutrients in them has to do with calculating daily requirements. We must go to charts of foods that list the average nutrient content and then balance what the dog could eat with what he needs. If each of the foods contained simply one nutrient, this calculation of diet balancing would be easier.

This has been a very basic introduction to nutrition. The six food requirements of water, carbohydrates, proteins, fats, vitamins and minerals provide the dog with everything he needs. Foods containing the right amounts of these nutrients must be eaten by the dog to balance with his particular body needs. Once eaten the food will be broken down and processed into usable forms for the many cells of the dog's body. This, very simply, is dog nutrition.

Wild and Ancestral Dog's Eating Habits

FAMINE

Hunter, hungry and active

FEAST

Sleep, full and inactive

The wild and ancestral dog's hunting and eating habits revolved around a feast or famine situation. As a hunter he was active both physically and mentally. Exercising his body and brain was important for survival. Once prey was captured and eaten it was time for rest and repair.. During this time there was no need or desire for exercise.

Our modern domesticated dog gets plenty of feasting and very little famine. Physical and mental activity is also limited. We have to consider this situation today and allow for exercise, maybe a little less feast and a little more famine. The dog should also avoid strenuous activity after eating. More on this later.

OUR PET'S BASIC DIGESTION AND ABSORPTION

Digestion refers to all the processes in which consumed foods are prepared within the dog's digestive system to be absorbed and used by his many cells. Food is required by the dog to furnish energy for body activities and for the building and repair of tissues. All foods, with the exception of water and minerals, are organic. Organic foods come either directly or indirectly from plants which have stored energy acquired from the sun. The dog obtains this energy directly if he consumers plant material and indirectly if he consumes animal products. Once consumed, the food material must be digested or broken down into usable forms before being absorbed for his own use.

The digestive process occurs within the dog's digestive system. This system consists of a tube with a few attachments or organs that break down the consumed food into usable form. Food enters at one end of the tube and, as it passes through, is transformed into absorbable products. The undigested is eliminated out the other end. This tube has adapted over millions of years to digest the dog's food.

Each part of the digestive system fulfills a specific task in the processing of the foods that enter the tube. The basic functions of the system include:

- the secretion of digestive enzymes,
- the movement of food materials, and
- the absorption of nutrients.

We shall discuss the parts of the digestive system and the duties each part performs.

The Digestion Tube

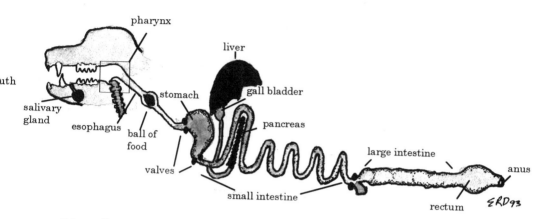

Mouth

The mouth includes lips, tongue, teeth, and salivary glands. The lips and tongue enable the dog to pick up and handle food, and the teeth, by tearing and chewing, provide some mechanical breakdown. The tongue can also taste so that undesirable foods and objects will not be swallowed. The salivary glands add saliva to the food which starts the digestion process, especially in young dogs. Saliva is also a lubricator that makes the swallowed food slippery, so that it will easily slide down the esophagus on its way to the stomach. Saliva also acts as a solvent, cleaning out the taste buds so that tasting of other foods can continue later on.

Pharynx

The pharynx is the area of the throat between the mouth and the esophagus. Here a flap, or valve, allows food to be swallowed when ready. The rest of the time, during breathing, air moves to and from the lungs.

Esophagus

The esophagus is a tube between the pharynx and stomach that is normally flattened except when a ball of food is being swallowed. Mucus is produced in this muscular tube, making it slippery. As the ball of food reaches the stomach a valve opens and the food enters the stomach. The valve closes to prevent food from coming back up.

Stomach

The stomach is a bag or pouch that is actually an enlargement in the digestive tube. In this bag, food is stored and the digestion process started. The process is triggered by the actions of gastric juices, primarily enzymes, hydrochloric acid and mucus. These special organic chemicals go to work breaking down the food into usable forms. Enzymes, for the most part, are made by the pancreas and small intestine. Dogs have a lot of one enzyme called gastric lipase in their stomachs, which is involved in fat digestion. The stomach also contains hydrochloric acid that helps in the digestion of food and may kill bad bacteria that could cause disease. Like the mouth and esophagus, mucus is also produced by the stomach wall, which lubricates and protects the lining of the stomach. We know that if an animal is under a lot of stress for a long time, too much acid may be produced and the walls may be eroded. These erosions or ulcers to the stomach wall can be troublesome.

Basically the stomach is a storage and digestion organ where very little absorption takes place. Some absorption of water and simple sugar or glucose may take place by tiny blood vessels in the walls of the stomach. The mixture of food and gastric juices in the stomach is called chyme, and at various intervals this mixture is "squirted" into the entrance to the small intestine where digestion will continue.

The dog's stomach will empty between meals, unlike the herbivore's stomach where food may remain for several days before moving on. Another difference is that the dog can vomit quite easily, as discussed before, compared to the horse for whom vomiting is virtually impossible. The cow, on the other hand, can bring up wads of food from her stomach, called a cud, which she can chew some more. This extra chewing helps her digest her particular kind of food. These differences remind us that the dog is a carnivore, and is built accordingly.

Small Intestine

The small intestine is a muscular tube that receives food from the stomach. It is here that the final phases of digestion and absorption of nutrients takes place. It has been said many times that the lining of the small intestine is one of the most remarkable organs of the body because of all the functions that it performs.

For the most part digestion is completed in the first section of the small intestine and absorption in the last section. Chyme that was squirted from the stomach came from an acid environment and is now in an alkaline or basic environment that allows for a different type of digestion to take place. Here in the small intestine, digestion will be completed with the aid of many different kinds of enzymes that originate primarily from the lining of the small intestine and pancreas. The pancreatic enzymes arrive through a tube or duct that empties near the front of the small intestine. Three main types of enzymes are at work in the small intestine breaking down carbohydrate, protein, and fat.

Near the duct from the pancreas, there is another duct that secrets bile from the liver, which also helps in the digestion of fat. This bile duct comes from the gall bladder and liver where bile is recycled and stored.

As the muscles of the small intestine push and pull the digesting food along, enzymes, bile and other secretions are doing their respective jobs in breaking down the food material. When nutrients become available in a usable form, they will be absorbed through the walls of the small intestine. The inside wall of the small intestine is not a smooth surface but rather a surface of many hills and valleys called villi. These villi provide up to seven or eight times more surface area for the absorption of nutrients.

Wall of the Small Intestine

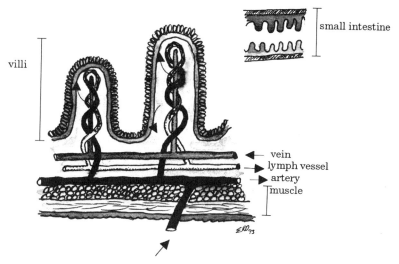

As the nutrients become acceptable for absorption, they are picked up by the blood and lymph. The majority of the nutrients are taken by the blood to various locations in the dog's body to be further processed or used directly. Lymph, a fluid of the lymphatic system, is another transportation system in the dog's body primarily involved with the fighting of disease. An example of something being absorbed by this system would be the absorption of antibody proteins in a puppy. These antibodies are present in the mother's milk, ready for use by the puppy to fight disease until he is able to make his own.

Foods that do not need to be broken down much are digested and absorbed quickly; more complex ones will take longer, and some will not be digested at all and will be passed out as feces.

This is a very simple explanation of a complex process of nutrients contained in foods making their way to the cells of the dog's body. As with any simplification, many facts and details are omitted, but let us realize that the small intestine is a very important and complex organ.

The small intestine of the dog is quite short compared to other animals. The length is about three and a half times the length of the dog's body. Because the dog is a carnivore, his intestine can be short as the food he has eaten for millions of years is relatively easy to digest. Other animals such as the cow which is a herbivore or vegetarian has a very long intestine. The cow's diet consists of coarse plant materials that are very hard to digest. The longer intestine allows for more room and time to digest this material. Furthermore, the cow has four stomachs and must rely on small microorganisms such as bacteria to help in the breakdown and digestion of this plant material.

Large Intestine

Next, the food moves into the large intestine. Most of the digestion and absorption has already taken place. As its name suggests, the diameter of the tube is larger than that of the small intestine. Again valves open and close between the two, and near this junction is a small pouch called a cecum. This pouch is the equivalent of the appendix in people. In herbivores the cecum is quite large and important as it permits the plant food to stay longer in the digestive system, thus allowing further microbial digestion. In the dog, however, the cecum is quite small and non-functional.

The main role of the large intestine in the dog is to absorb and conserve water. If a dog is short of drinking water for some time or has lost water due to exercise or hot weather, his stools will be hard and dry. This is the result of his body conserving as much water as it can. There is also a great amount of mucus production in the large intestine to lubricate and protect the walls from this dried out fecal material.

Rectum and Anus

The rectum is the end of the digestion tube and is the storage facility for all undigested material. This undigested material, feces, is stored here until a time is suitable for removal through the last valve, the anus.

We have discussed in very simple terms the digestion tube, which takes in swallowed food at one end, digesting and absorbing nutrients as the food is pushed along to the other end. We note that there are major differences between the digestive systems of carnivores, or predominantly meat eaters and herbivores, and plant eaters, which we must remember when feeding our dog.

In addition to this digestion and absorption tube, there are two very important organs, the pancreas and the liver. These two, along with the stomach and the small intestine, are the central digesting and processing machinery involved in the conversion of food to a form that can be utilized by the cells of the dog. Before we leave the digestive system we must discuss these two very important organs.

Pancreas

The pancreas is a gland situated near the beginning of the the small intestine. It performs two main functions: the production of digestive enzymes, and the formation of two hormones, insulin and glucagon, which are involved in the regulation of blood sugar.

Enzymes are internal organic catalysts. These chemical substances are made in the pancreas and are able to stimulate a specific chemical reaction without themselves entering into the reaction or undergoing any change. Enzymes are present in tiny amounts and can either promote the breakdown of complex organic compounds or stimulate the formation of other compounds. Each enzyme has one very specific function that it performs.

Many enzymes have been discovered and identified to date, and there are probably still more to be discovered. The digestive enzymes are manufactured primarily in the pancreas and small intestine. An example of an enzyme produced in the small intestine is the enzyme lactase, which acts upon the milk sugar lactose. Lactase reduces or breaks down lactose in milk into simpler sugars that the puppy can utilize for energy. There is less lactose in the nursing puppy's milk than in cow's milk and since lactase may not be present in the adult dog, giving cow's milk to a dog can cause diarrhea. The puppy may not have enough of this enzyme and the adult may not have any, so cow's milk is passed only partially digested and is fermented by bacteria in the large intestine. Yogurt, on the other hand, can be digested and is a good protein source for the young and adult dog.

The other function of the pancreas is the production of insulin and glucagon. These two hormones regulate the amount of blood sugar, called glucose, circulating in the blood.

Insulin makes the glucose in the blood and tissues more readily available for use as energy by the cells. Without insulin, blood glucose levels rise because the cells are not willing to use the glucose. This disease from lack of insulin production by the pancreas is called diabetes mellitus (mellitus meaning honey, or sweet). When dogs have this problem, they are excessively thirsty and frequently urinate as their bodies attempt to lower this high blood sugar level.

The other hormone made by the pancreas is glucagon. Glucagon functions in the breakdown of liver glycogen, or animal starch, to glucose for energy. This will be discussed further in the section on carbohydrates.

Liver

The liver is the largest gland in the dog's body and is essential to life. Of all animals, the dog has the largest liver at three percent of his body weight. Puppies' livers are even larger. This large size is due to the dog's carnivorous diet. A large liver is required to metabolize the high concentration of protein and fat.

This important complex organ and gland is made up of a group of specialized cells. Their main purpose is to release certain substances and to separate and eliminate other substances. Some of the functions that the liver performs are:

- the formation and storage of animal starch (glycogen)
- the secretion of bile (for fat digestion)
- the detoxification of poisons
- the breakdown of uric acid and the formation of urea (from protein digestion) and
- the breakdown of fatty acids (from fat digestion).

The liver is also involved in the storage of vitamins, the destruction of old red blood cells and the formation of blood proteins. As we can see from this long list, the liver is a complex and important organ. It is believed that the liver is also a site of hormone production for the regulation of the complex digestive processes.

The large liver of the dog is kept busy digesting the food he has eaten and processing the nutrients into a form that his cells can use.

In summary we have looked at the digestive system as a modified tube with two accessory organs, the pancreas and the liver. Whole food is taken in at one end; the "good stuff" is taken out, and the rest passes through.

We must, however, appreciate how important and complex the digestive system is. We must also appreciate that the dog is a carnivore and his digestive system has suited him well on this type of diet for millions of years. That is, his teeth are primarily used for tearing and ripping, he has the ability to vomit easily, his intestines are short and his liver is large and effective. These are all characteristics that have permitted the dog to live and survive on his predominantly animal flesh diet. These are all considerations we must bear in mind when we cook for and feed our dog.

We shall now discuss the food groups and nutrients in greater detail with regard to body functions, food sources, and deficiency problems.

"Almost any function that occurs within a dog's body has some dependency on water."

Donald R. Collins, DVM, *The Collins Guide to Dog Nutrition*

Water is the most important nutrient of all. Without water life cannot continue. Back to the illustration of the teeter-totter.

If water were not available the dog would die within a very short time as very little water is stored in the dog's body. It has been observed that if a dog loses one tenth of his water it will die. The dog will normally drink enough water to meet his own requirements. An average sized dog of about forty pounds must take in a little more than a liter or quart of water every day. About half of this he will get from the food he eats and the rest from drinking. If he eats only dry dog food then he must drink to get most of his daily requirement. Scientists say that the dog will drink about ten times a day, so water should always be available.

Greater than seventy percent of the dog's total body weight is water, but the daily amount required will vary greatly. It will vary with the individual dog, his environment, and his activity. If, for example, he is very active and the weather is hot, then much more water is consumed, because water is needed for the cells as they burn up energy and also for the removal of heat. If a mother is nursing puppies she needs more water, as would a dog sick with fever, diarrhea, or kidney disease.

We should have lots of fresh clean water available at all times. Other things to consider are the mineral content and temperature of this water. Too warm or too cold may discourage the dog from drinking as much as he needs.

How would we know if our dog is not getting enough water? He would have hard, dry, foul smelling stools, and as the deficiency continues, he would show signs of dehydration. His eyes would become sunk into their sockets, his nose would be dry, and he would be thirsty. If he is a short haired individual, when we pinched his skin on his neck, the skin would stay in a fold for several seconds. These are signs of serious dehydration and we should have him looked at by a veterinarian as soon as possible.

Severe dehydration can occur with sickness such as fever, diarrhea or heat stroke. Young puppies are especially vulnerable to dehydration and may be so dehydrated that water given orally may not be enough, and intravenous fluids maybe necessary if the dog is to live.

Water fulfills many needs for the dog. It is an excellent solvent and is the main component of blood. Water provides transportation for blood, nutrients, antibodies, and waste. Temperature regulation such as heat loss due to evaporation and removal of heat from internal organs out to the skin surface is another function that water provides. Lastly, water is essential for digestion and urine production. We cannot over-emphasize the importance of water.

Normally water is lost through the expired air, feces, and urine. The dog's skin doesn't perspire like ours, so when he is hot, he will pant to get rid of excess heat. Heat can be lost through the pads of his paws as some perspiration occurs here.

Have clean fresh water available for the dog at all times, especially when his environment is hot.

A dog eats to fulfill his energy requirements. The food he eats contains stored energy that originated from the sun. He obtains this energy directly if he eats plant material, and indirectly when he eats animal material.

The food the dog has eaten, containing this stored energy, is first digested and absorbed by his digestive system. Later it is metabolized or changed within the many cells of the dog. In the cells, energy is used or released. This metabolism, be it either a breakdown process or a building process, occurs within the tissues and results in energy used for heat or work.

Energy is required for many things:

- to maintain body temperature,
- for vital activities;
    - heart beating and blood circulation,
    - breathing,
    - all internal body functions such as digestion,
- for the growth and repair of body tissues,
- for muscular activity, like running and play,

Energy is the "bottom line" and like water is an essential item for all living things.

Nutrients such as carbohydrates, fats, and proteins all supply energy. The unit for measuring energy is the calorie. Some foods contain more calories than others and some none at all. For example a unit of fat has 2.2 times the number of calories as the same unit of carbohydrate or protein. Only carbohydrates, fats, and proteins contain energy or calories. Water, vitamins and minerals do not.

The amount of energy or calories required per day by an individual dog will vary. Generally, each individual dog has different energy requirements and the number of calories needed everyday will vary with:

- Age; young require more than old
- Breed; large dogs require more than small dogs
- Pregnancy and lactation increases energy requirements
- Intact; more than spayed or neutered
- Activity; running more than sleeping
- Environment; Cold more than warm surroundings
- Emotion; excitement, worry, more than calm, and relaxed.

From this long list we can readily appreciate how one individual could have a much greater need for calories than another.

For example: a young, active, pregnant female in an outside run during the winter, would require many more calories than an old neutered male living in a warm apartment. This is an extreme example, but it illustrates the point that caloric requirements vary with the individual dog in the particular circumstance.

In formulating diets, the first consideration is balancing the available energy content of the food with the daily energy needs of the particular dog. Energy, like water, is very important and if the intake is inadequate the dog will soon start losing weight as his body stores are being used. However, if the energy intake is more than the dog requires for his daily needs, his body will store the excess as body fat and save it for another time when he may be short. Thus, there is a need for balance: not enough will result in weight loss and too much will result in gain. If either of these situations continue for long, the outcome is starvation or obesity.

By running our hand over his ribs we can get a fairly good idea of the dog's body condition. If we can feel every rib then he is short of energy; if we cannot maybe he has had too much.

Carbohydrates are the main source of energy, or calories, for almost all mammals, including people. These foods are of plant origin and include vegetables, fruits, pulses, and grains. We know that the dog has lived for millions of years as a carnivore eating very little carbohydrate, except when he ate the stomach contents of his prey. The dog can make energy from protein and fats, as we all can. In the book, *The Clever Coyote*, authors Young and Jackson, compiled many extensive studies of the North American coyote for the Wildlife Management Institute, in Washington, D.C. These studies go back as far as the early 1900's. The stomach contents of over fifty thousand coyotes were examined. The research found that the coyote, or wild North American cousin of our domestic dog, is for the most part a pure carnivore. That is to say the coyote's diet consisted almost entirely of animals and birds, insects and fish. Very little plant material was found except for berries and fruit depending upon the area and season. These dogs of the wild obtained their dietary energy primarily from proteins and fats, as true carnivores with "second-hand" carbohydrates.

This as we have said before, could explain the dog's relatively large liver and short intestine. The larger liver allows a greater capacity for processing the proteins and fats into energy.

We have made our modern dog into an omnivore, in that we give him carbohydrate foods such as grains and vegetables. Because these kinds of foods are used for dietary sources of energy in the modern dog diet, we shall discuss carbohydrates in more detail. Carbohydrates provide a source of less expensive short term energy than proteins. If we were discussing a strict carnivore diet, we would not emphasize carbohydrates as a calorie source.

We have learned that many carbohydrates can be used by the dog. We have also learned that it is important to breakdown these foods before we give them to the dog. For example, grains and vegetables should be cooked or baked first, to aid digestion. Large amounts of raw carbohydrates may lead to diarrhea and flatulence, probably due to fermentation by bacteria in the large intestine.

As we have stated, carbohydrates are the prime source of calories in almost all diets with the exception of the true carnivore. Simple carbohydrates are called sugars and more complex are referred to as starches. They are also called monosaccharides and polysaccharides. Saccharides are sugar molecules, mono meaning single, and poly meaning many. A list, with examples may help explain.

Monosaccharide	single sugar	glucose, fructose (fruit sugar)
Disaccharide	two sugars	sucrose (table sugar,) or glucose and fructose,
Polysaccharide	many sugars	starches. (potatoes)

Polysaccharides, or starches, are several chains of single sugars interlinked one with another. The digestive system with its enzymes must break these down into single sugars, before they can be absorbed and utilized by the cells. Microorganisms, like bacteria, help in this breakdown of starches in herbivores such as the cow and horse. Because dogs do not have a digestive system suited for these microorganisms, they cannot digest many of these starches and so they pass on through. This material we refer to as fiber or roughage. Fiber can be polysaccharides such as cellulose which makes up the main structure of plant cell walls and is almost impossible for the dog to digest. This fiber can bind water and adds bulk to the stools.

The wild dog obtained his roughage or fiber from the prey he ate. These dogs would consume the whole animal or bird, including the hair and feathers. This acted as the "fiber" part of their diet which would "bulk-up" the feces and also protected the intestinal walls from sharp things such as fragments of bone. The hair, feathers and other materials. formed a coating to the stool protecting the intestinal walls from these sharp pieces.

Let's look again at digestion of carbohydrates. The sugars and starches that are consumed must first be broken down to single sugars such a glucose before the intestine can absorb this material. Once absorbed through the walls of the intestine, blood picks up the glucose and transports it to where it can be:

- Used by the cells directly for energy,
- Converted in the liver to glycogen (animal starch)
  then stored as liver glycogen, or
  stored in the muscles as muscle glycogen,
- Converted in the liver into fat and stored on the body
  as body fat, or,
- Excreted through the kidneys.

Glucose is usually the only simple sugar circulating in the blood. The liver is very important at this point in that it can take glucose and store it for a while or convert it to glycogen or fat. The liver can also convert these back to blood glucose if the need for energy should arise later.

Muscle glycogen, the stored form of glucose in the muscle, is used only by the muscles and cannot go back to the liver to be recycled. As the glycogen is used in the muscles, one of the by-products formed is a substance called lactic acid. If there is a lot of this material formed, for example after a big work out, the dog will be stiff and sore. Only after the lactic acid is either sent back to the liver, or converted back to glycogen by more blood glucose will the stiffness subside.

The liver is the main storage organ for blood glucose. If a dog is starving, the glucose will last for about twenty-four to forty-eight hours, and then body fat will have to be converted back to blood glucose and energy.

These chemical reactions back and forth are all referred to as carbohydrate metabolism with glucose as the main carbohydrate utilized for energy in the body, and glycogen, or animal starch, the main storage form.

The amount of blood glucose circulating in the dog's body is regulated by hormones. If there is too much, the pancreas will release insulin which will make the cells accept more glucose. If there is still too much, it may be removed by the kidneys and excreted in the urine. If the blood glucose is too low - this is called hypoglycemia - the adrenal gland will release adrenalin (as well as glucagon from the pancreas) to activate the liver to release more glucose or to make more from its stores of liver glycogen. This "shot" of adrenalin and the resulting quick burst of energy is very important for the "Fight or Flight" mechanism and the dog's ultimate survival, if he should be confronted with danger.

All cells require energy as we have said, and brain cells are no exception. If anything, the brain is especially vulnerable to low blood glucose levels. Glucose can readily pass from the blood to the brain. We know, for example, if we feel tired and listless, we can get a quick "lift" by eating a chocolate bar. The sugars in the bar are quickly absorbed into the blood and transported to the cells of the brain for energy. This is also true with the dog, so if we have an active dog and he appears listless between meals, maybe a small treat is in order.

Proteins are the building blocks for the dog's body. They are also the most complex molecules found in nature. Things like hair, hooves, muscle, and hormones are classified as proteins. Proteins are made up of simpler compounds called amino acids. Of these amino acids twenty-three have been known to modern science for some time. Thirteen can be manufactured in the dog's body, from digested protein while the other ten, called essential amino acids, must be present on a regular basis in the food the dog eats. This list is changing as modern science learns more.

A diet must have several different proteins in it to ensure that the dog gets all the amino acids he needs. Foods such as meat, fish, eggs and dairy products contain large amounts of the essential amino acids. Vegetable source proteins may be short of some essential amino acids, so it becomes important to feed a combination of foods that will include all the essentials.

Proteins are quickly digested or broken down into the simpler amino acids. These are then absorbed and go either to be broken down further in the liver or to the cells of the body to be used for growth or repair. Newly made proteins in the body are classified into structural or functional proteins. Muscle is structural and insulin is functional. Unlike carbohydrates and fats, proteins are not stored in the dog's body for very long. In an adult dog that is "stable", not gaining or losing weight, the amount of protein eaten will be equal to the amount removed or excreted as waste. This is called Nitrogen Balance. An exception to this would be a growing puppy that is using more protein to grow muscles and other cells. Other examples would be a nursing mother dog or a dog getting over an injury. Any excess protein eaten not used for growth or repair is either used for energy, stored as fat or removed as waste.

Because of this nitrogen balance and the fact that proteins not used cannot be stored, it is important that the dog eat quality protein on a regular basis.

There are many different things that proteins do in the dog's body. They are involved in the formation of muscle, tendons, hormones, enzymes and antibodies. Proteins form the bulk of the organic compounds in all cells. They are used in the formation of new cells and the repair and restoration of cells that already exist. Protein not used for new cells or repair of other cells is broken down in the liver, kidney and muscle into energy or waste. The energy can be used or stored as fat, and the waste, ammonia, is excreted in the urine.

Excess protein is used for energy as is carbohydrate and fat, but carbohydrate and fat cannot be used as protein. Protein must be eaten as protein. The use of the dog's body protein as a source of energy during starvation can be done for a short period of time but will rapidly result in permanent damage or death. In other words the dog's body is consuming itself and not its reserves as with body fat. To repeat, protein must be regularly present in the diet.

A dog's daily diet must contain enough of the right kind of protein if he is to survive and be healthy. The amount of protein a dog will need every day will depend on how well the protein can supply his needs for amino acids. The ability of the protein to do this is called biological value. Foods of high biological value are those with many of the essential amino acids present in them. Eggs and fish meal have a high biological value, for example, and foods like rice and wheat gluten have a low biological value. This knowledge becomes important in balancing the dog's requirements for protein.

Protein is an important nutrient that must be eaten regularly and cannot be replaced by anything else.

Fats provide energy. This nutrient fulfills other needs but the primary one is as a concentrated form of energy. Within the body, fat can be stored to be used as energy later if the need should arise. Body fat offers padding for organs, such as the heart, kidneys and eyes. as well as giving contour, or shape to the dog's body. Fat is also very good insulation against cold temperatures.

The principal function, however, for fats may be the part they play in the production of substances vital to the internal workings of the dog. Fat is a major part of the walls of all body cells, especially brain and nerve cells. Fat is also necessary in the digestion and processing of other nutrients, particularly proteins.

Fat in a dog's diet serves many functions:

- Provides a source of concentrated energy
- Supplies essential fatty acids
- Acts as a carrier for fat soluble vitamins
- Adds palatability or taste

All dietary fats are made up of triglycerides. Triglycerides consist of three fatty acids and a unit of glycerol. Different fatty acids give a fat its particular characteristics. There are dozens of fatty acids known to us today and we classify them into two basic groups;

- Saturated, or hard fats from animal sources, such as lard and butter,
- Polyunsaturated, liquid, or soft fats from vegetable sources.

Dogs can utilize fats from either animal or plant sources. The digestibility of fats will vary with the source and the processing. Fat also can become rancid and undesirable. More on this later when we discuss commercial dog food.

Fatty acids known as linoleic and linolenic acids are considered to be essential, in that they cannot be manufactured in the dog's body. They must be eaten. These two plus arachidonic acid make up the base for the production of other fatty acids that are important to his everyday life.

Among the vital substances made in the body from the essential fatty acids are a group of organic substances called Prostaglandins. Lately, in human medicine, it is thought that Prostaglandins and faulty fatty acid metabolism may have something to do with many of man's chronic health problems such as heart disease, cancer, allergies, and obesity.

Fat eaten by the dog is broken down by enzymes into fatty acids and glycerol. After absorption, the fatty acids are either used to manufacture vital substances or to build or repair cell walls. The glycerol is used for energy.

A dog deficient in the essential fatty acids will have coarse dry hair, rough hard skin, impaired growth, and loss of muscle tone. Hair loss may also occur, especially on the abdomen, inside the thighs, and between the shoulder blades.

All excess fat consumed will be stored in the form of body fat. These stores are available for the dog to use later when starvation or food for energy is not available. We have said before that carbohydrates and proteins can also be converted to body fat stores. Something we must note is that the dog's body will go on storing or saving this energy as fat continually. The dog will get "fatter and fatter" as he saves more and more. There seems to be no limit as to how obese a dog can get.

In other words, too many calories end up in fat. For every 3000 - 3500 excess calories consumed, the dog will put on about one pound of body fat. To remove body fat, the intake of calories must be lowered to below the daily requirements, so that body stores will be used, resulting in a reduction in the dog's body weight. If the dog requires more calories due to a lot of exercise, for example, these reserves can be used.

Simply put: "calories in should equal calories out". The dog should be fed enough calories to supply his daily needs. Any more than that requirement will end up as body fat. Any less and the dog will use body fat. Too rapid a loss of body fat can sometime result in a condition called Ketosis. The liver is not able to completely convert the body fat back to glucose and ketones are formed. These ketones will give the dog an acetone smelling breath and loss of appetite. Rapid weight loss diets can cause this condition and veterinary help is advised.

Fat is an important nutrient performing many important functions as well as being a powerful energy fuel. When we come to the section on working dogs, fat will be an important ingredient because of its concentrated energy. Fat has received a lot of publicity lately. It is blamed for many problems in people, but as with so many things we must look at the whole picture. To isolate one nutrient out of many without regards for the interaction of all in a living body in a particular environment, is often a mistake.

VITAMINS

Vitamins are vital organic food substances necessary in small amounts for normal metabolism and growth of the dog. Vitamins help regulate the chemical reactions that protect cells and aid in the conversion of food into energy and living tissue. Everyday we hear more about these vital substances and how they are involved in many areas of nutrition. Vitamins are similar to enzymes, in that they are present in very small amounts performing their metabolic functions, but differ in that they are not produced in the body. They must be in the diet.

Scientists have so far identified thirteen of these organic substances that we call vitamins. In 1911 a scientist named Hopkins realized that there was something else present in foods besides carbohydrates, proteins, and fats that was required for health. He referred to these nutrients as "accessory food factors". The next year, Funk discovered a nitrogen factor in yeast and rice polishings that cured beriberi (a muscular paralysis, seen in people eating a diet high in polished rice.) This he called vitamine (life amine) later to be called Vitamin B_1 or Thiamine. Accessory food factors or vitamins were soon realized to be essential nutrients.

The vitamins were given letters of the alphabet and classified into those soluble in fat: A, D, E, and K and those soluble in water such as B and C. Later it was discovered that there was more than one substance involved with some of these, so they were given numbers, for example B_1, B_6 or B_{12}. I am sure there are more to be discovered and identified in the future.

After their discovery, vitamins were used to prevent deficiency problems such as scurvy, beriberi, and rickets. Today's scientists are looking at the use of vitamins in maintaining optimal health and preventing some diseases.

Some of the latest vitamin research in human health has to do with the antioxidant properties of Vitamins E, C, and beta carotene (vitamin A base). Antioxidants are able to deactivate harmful substances such as free radicals. Free radicals are chemically reactive substances that have combined with oxygen when the body is exposed to things like x-rays, sunlight, tobacco smoke, car exhaust, and other environmental pollutants. Free radicals can damage DNA, alter chemical compounds, corrode cell membranes and kill cells outright. Scientists think this kind of damage leads to cancer, heart and lung disease and cataracts. By consuming natural antioxidants that will attach to the free radicals making them harmless, perhaps some diseases can be prevented. Another benefit may be in delaying the many problems associated with aging. A lot of the human vitamin research can apply to the dog and we will be hearing more.

Questions arise when feeding our dog: does he need vitamins, and is he getting these vitamins? Yes, dogs require vitamins just as we do. Many years ago he obtained his vitamins from the various foods that he ate as he roamed the countryside. However, as we had stated earlier, his diet and environment has changed radically. Today's dog is often limited to processed foods, thus other questions must be asked. For example, what does the heat of processing do to the vitamin content of the original food ingredients? What does the addition of preservatives do to the vitamins? Should we be feeding a variety of fresh foods so that he gets the vitamins that he requires, both known and unknown to modern science?

Could there be other important factors involved in the way nutrients act within the dog's body that are still unknown? We also have a dog in an environment that has chemical products from car exhaust to carpet shampoos that are totally new to him. In other words our modern dog has a limited diet and different surroundings to contend with. On top of all of this he has no choice!

What are the dog's vitamin requirements? There are tables and recommendations made from studies of dogs fed different diets.

As with people, feeding recommendations are made for the average individual in average conditions. The recommendations are for the prevention of vitamin deficiencies, but, as we had stated earlier, scientists are now looking beyond this and using vitamins for treatment.

It has been stated that, in general, the vitamin requirements are related to the intake of energy. If energy intake is increased, then vitamin intake should increase. A growing puppy or a nursing mother dog, for example, would require more energy and also more vitamins. However, older dogs do not need as much energy although the latest research may indicate that they may require more vitamins.

The amounts of vitamins consumed and actually utilized by the dog may vary greatly depending upon many factors. For example, several vitamins are unstable, and their destruction may be promoted by light, heat, oxidation, moisture, rancidity, or certain minerals. It is important to note, however, that feeding excessive amounts of some vitamins will cause overdoses. Vitamins are an interesting and ever changing topic with recommendations on requirements changing everyday.

To feed our dog today, we should have a basic understanding of vitamins: what they do, what foods contain them, and how we might detect a shortage. With this knowledge we may be better equipped to evaluate our dog's diet and his health.

We are going to list the individual vitamins with information on what that vitamin does in the body, what signs we may see if the vitamin is deficient or overdosed and some food sources.

Vitamin A has long been known to be an important vitamin in human and animal nutrition. Generally speaking, vitamin A is important for epithelial cells. These cells are responsible for the internal and external surfaces of the body including skin, eyes, lungs and uterus.

Deficiencies of vitamin A will show up as dry skin and eyes and general poor growth and development. Night blindness is a common condition from a lack of sufficient vitamin A. The old saying "eat carrots if you want to see in the dark," has basis in scientific fact as the yellow pigment or carotene in carrots is necessary for the body to manufacture vitamin A.

For many years, livestock people have been aware of the importance of vitamin A for their farm livestock. Most farm animals make their vitamin A from green grass, but during the winter, when green grass is not available, they must be supplemented.

Vitamin A is only found in animal products and is made from carotenes or the yellow pigments in plants. Beta cartotene is the most important carotene and is water soluble. Because vitamin A is fat soluble and can be stored in fat, excess can be toxic, whereas beta carotene, the plant source ingredient for vitamin A, is water soluble and excess is excreted through the urine.

The best food sources for vitamin A are liver, egg yolks, butter, and whole milk. Best sources for beta carotene are dark green leafy vegetables, yellow and orange vegetables and fruits.

As we continue to go through the food sources for the vitamins, liver will be listed as a food source for all the vitamins. Some nutritionists call liver the "perfect food" for this reason. One of the first things eaten by the wild carnivore is the liver of its prey. So maybe they know this as well. We will list many recipes with liver as an ingredient, but must always beware not to feed too much, as excesses of the fat soluble vitamins can cause serious problems. Too much vitamin A, for example, can lead to impaired vision, skin rashes, hair loss, and liver damage.

To summarize, vitamin A is an important essential vitamin that can be obtained from animal sources. Beta carotene, one of the main ingredients for vitamin A manufacture, is acquired from plant sources. Too much vitamin A is trouble, and not enough will result in signs of poor growth, dry skin, eye problems, as well as lung and reproductive problems.

Vitamins in general are required in such small amounts that the signs of a deficiency may take some time before we suspect a problem. A dog could carry on for a long time on limited amounts of some vitamins, which is not the case with some other nutrients.

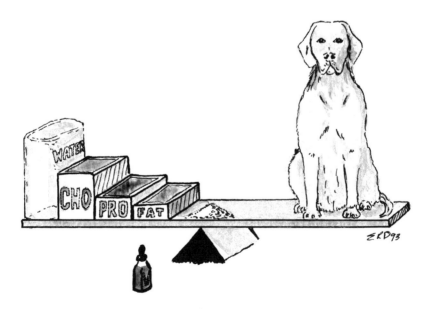

The balance drops only slightly when we remove the vitamins.

Vitamin D, another fat soluble vitamin, is a vital factor in calcium and phosphorus metabolism of the dog. These three are essential for the formation of bones and teeth. We can get most of our vitamin D from sun exposure on our skin, as well as our diet. The dog's skin is covered with hair, however, so he must obtain his from his food. The relationship between Vitamin D, calcium and phosphorus, is quite delicate with regard to the amounts of each. Too much of one or the other or a shortage of any one can throw this relationship off and problems will arise.

Conditions like rickets, soft bones, enlargement of joints, and late appearing teeth can result. Older dogs will show signs of bone pain and broken bones. New mothers may have eclampsia, a form of paralysis, shortly after whelping. All are related to vitamin D.

Vitamin D is present in liver, butter, fatty fish, fish oils, egg yolks, and fortified milk. Too much vitamin D can result in calcium deposits throughout the dog's body, as well as fatigue, vomiting and diarrhea.

Vitamin D, calcium and phosphorus are important considerations in growing puppies, especially the giant breeds such as Great Danes and St. Bernards. Because these puppies are growing so fast, these three nutrients become very important. If you are raising puppies from the large breeds, seek professional assistance in formulating their diet, as this is beyond the scope of this book.

Because vitamins, like minerals, are required in such small amounts, it may take some time for signs of shortage to appear.

Vitamin E

Vitamin E is actually a group of compounds called tocopherols. Tocopherols are all fat soluble and their absorption from the intestine depends upon digestion and absorption of fat. Vitamin E also functions with the mineral selenium. Both of these are involved in muscle growth and repair, and as anti-oxidants.

As we discussed previously, living tissues are sensitive to the damaging effects of oxygen and other oxidizing substances called free radicals. Nature, in its wisdom, has provided a substance to protect cells against the free radicals of oxidation. They are the anti-oxidants. Vitamin E, C, beta-carotene, and selenium containing amino acids are nature's anti-oxidants.

Vitamin E is found in liver, most vegetable oils, nuts, seeds, fish oil, as well as eggs and dairy products. Many fats and oils, when combined with oxygen in the atmosphere and exposed to heat and light, can become rancid. Vitamin E, an anti-oxidant, can retard this process, by acting as a preservative. This is nature's way of preserving fats and oils from going rancid.

To summarize, Vitamin E plays an important role as an anti-oxidant and free radical fighter. Deficiencies result in muscular dystrophy like conditions in puppies and reproductive problems in the adults. Too much can cause stomach upsets.

Vitamin K is important for the production of blood clotting factors. Factors, especially one called prothrombin, clot blood if the dog is cut or injured. A deficiency of vitamin K is quite rare and can produce bleeding disorders. Sometimes the diet of newborn or premature puppies may be supplemented with vitamin K. Vitamin K is given to a dog that has been poisoned with warfarin, an anti-coagulant and common rodent poison. Warfarin, prevents the rodent's blood from clotting, eventually killing it.

Foods such as liver, meat, leafy vegetables, corn and soybean oil and dairy products contain vitamin K. Excesses are especially dangerous for puppies, in that their livers may be overloaded. As said before, Vitamin K shortages are rare.

This concludes our discussion of the four fat soluble vitamins, A,D,E, and K. Because these four are fat soluble, we must be careful that the dog does not get too much. This can happen if a dog develops a taste for a particular food, and we only give him this one food. Liver is a good example. If we only fed liver, it would not take long before the dog would be in trouble from too much of a good thing. The old saying, "If a little is good a lot should be better" is not true in this case.

We must be sure that the dog has enough vitamins, however, to supply his needs. A deficency of vitamins, unlike water and energy, may not become evident for some time. It is important that we rely on variety, knowledge and quality foods when we feed our dog.

B Vitamins

The B vitamins, of which eight are known, are a group of essential nutrients with many common characteristics. They are all water soluble and usually found in the same foods including brewer's yeast, meat, whole grain cereals, and vegetable proteins. Chemically the eight B vitamins are distinct, but their functions are quite similar. Rarely would we see a deficiency of just one but rather a combination of several; therefore, usually a B complex supplement would be given to a dog. B vitamins are generally involved with muscle, skin and blood.

Vitamin B_1 [Thiamin]

Thiamin was one of the first vitamins discovered, in connection with beriberi and people eating polished rice. Vitamin B_1 is found in skeletal muscle, heart muscle, brain, kidney, and liver. Any deficiency will result in deterioration of these tissues. Thiamin plays an important role in energy production and carbohydrate metabolism, as do all the B vitamins.

There are a number of naturally occurring anti-vitamins of thiamin called thiaminases that can modify thiamin and lead to signs of deficiencies. Foods like raw fish, shellfish, ferns, bacteria, yeast, and fungi have thiaminases. Heat will destroy these anti-vitamins, so it is recommended that we cook fish before we feed it to the dog.

Signs of thiamin deficiency in the dog include general weakness, vomiting, unsteadiness, especially of the hind legs, acute heart failure, and death.

Even though Thiamin is a water soluble vitamin and we do not have to worry as much with overdosing as we do with fat soluble vitamins previously discussed, thiamin toxicity has been seen in the dog. So, as with all vitamins, a little is fine; too much may be trouble.

Vitamin B$_2$ [Riboflavin]

Riboflavin was first discovered in the 1930's and plays an important role manufacturing enzymes in the liver. Enzymes are important in the metabolism of carbohydrate, protein, and fat.

Vitamin B$_2$ is closely related to Vitamin B$_6$ and both are found in milk, cereals, meats, liver, and some leafy green vegetables. This vitamin will deteriorate in these foods when the foods are exposed to light; however, cooking will not effect it.

Deficiency may result in loss of weight, muscular weakness in the hind legs, dermatitis, and red tearing eyes. Riboflavin is especially important in growing puppies, pregnant and nursing mothers and in older dogs.

Vitamin B$_3$ [Niacin]

Niacin deficiency has long been known to cause pellagra in man and blacktongue in the dog. Besides an inflamed tongue, the dog will show weight loss, loss of appetite, foul breath, and blood stained drooling from the mouth. Bloody diarrhea may be another sign that this vitamin is lacking in the diet.

Vitamin B$_3$, as with the other B vitamins, is important in the formation of certain enzymes involved with carbohydrate metabolism. The amino acid tryptophan is required for the manufacture of niacin which explains why dogs on a high corn diet may have this deficiency. Corn protein is known to be low in tryptophan.

Foods sources include meat, particularly beef, milk, fish and whole grains. Dogs particularly susceptible are those with a poor protein intake or high corn diet.

Vitamin B$_5$ [Pantothenic Acid]

This is one of the lesser B vitamins, found in most foods, but more so in eggs, whole grain cereals and meat. Vitamin B$_5$ has the same general duties in the metabolism of energy and shows the same signs of deficiencies as the other B vitamins. When B vitamins are a concern in the diet, usually all the B vitamins will be supplemented.

Medical people tell us that with the B vitamins deficiency, signs will show up as mental changes first. Signs like irritability, nervousness, and insomnia are examples in humans. We may also be observing these signs in dogs, which might be from a deficiency of the B vitamins.

Vitamin B$_6$ [Pyridoxine]

Vitamin B$_6$ plays a major role in the metabolism of proteins. Dogs on high protein diets require more Vitamin B$_6$. There is also a relationship with vitamin B$_2$ and magnesium. B$_6$ is important with several body chemicals involved in the brain and has been associated with mood and behavior in man.

Good food sources include meat, fish, egg yolk, whole grain cereals, bananas and nuts. Cottage cheese is low in B$_6$. Linseed meal (from flaxseed) contains linatine which will deactivate vitamin B$_6$, so we should beware of this potential problem if we should decide to give our dog flaxseed, which is an old time supplement.

Deficiencies result in loss of appetite, slow growth and weight loss. Epileptic type convulsions, skin inflammation and hair loss have also been seen with vitamin B$_6$ deficiency.

Vitamin B$_{12}$ [cyanocobalamin]

Vitamin B$_{12}$ is only found in animal tissue. This vitamin plays an important role in the manufacture of red blood cells. Deficiencies appear as anemia, or thinning of the blood due to a decrease in the number of red blood cells circulating in the body. Red blood cells carry oxygen to all of the other cells. If their numbers are down, the skin around the eyes and mouth will appear pale, and the dog will tire easily.

Good food sources are liver, organ meats, meat, and to a lesser extent, fish, eggs, and brewers yeast. Stores of vitamin B$_{12}$ can last for many years.

Folic Acid

Folic acid is closely linked to vitamin B$_{12}$ and is essential in the workings of the nervous system. This vitamin is destroyed by cooking, and deficiency symptoms are generally the same: anemia, shortness of breath and pale skin.

Food sources include liver, green vegetables, kidneys, eggs and whole grain cereals. Dairy products contain little Folic acid.

Biotin

Biotin is a lesser known B vitamin, and deficiencies appear as a scaly skin condition in the dog. Biotin is present in meats, dairy products, and whole grain cereals. Raw egg whites have a protein, avidin, which binds biotin making it ineffective. If we were to feed our dog the odd raw egg, this would not be a problem, but if we should feed a lot for some length of time, he could develop a Biotin deficiency. A dog on antibiotics or sulfa drug treatment for an extended period of time may also show deficiencies of biotin.

Vitamin C [Ascorbic Acid]

Lack of vitamin C in humans has long been known to cause a bleeding disorder called scurvy. This was a problem for the British Navy in the seventeenth and eighteenth centuries when access to fresh fruits and vegetables was limited. Due to the amount of publicity that Vitamin C receives today regarding the common cold as well as the prevention and treatment of many disorders, it has become the most widely consumed nutritional supplement.

The popular consensus is that the dog produces his own ascorbic acid or vitamin C. Some studies have shown that there may be a big variation between individuals, especially during times of stress. As a result, many veterinarians are prescribing vitamin C.

For all of us, vitamin C is essential for the formation of collagen, a cementing substance, that binds the many cells of connective tissue. Collagen is found in skin, tendons, bones, teeth and joints of all kinds. It is also in blood vessels and muscles. Vitamin C then becomes important in wound healing and repair of tissues.

Vitamin C is alleged to be beneficial in preventing and treating many conditions such as allergies, cataracts, diabetes and cancer. It also has an important relationship to the immune system and stress.

Most fresh fruits and green vegetables, liver, kidney and potatoes are good food sources. Being water soluble, vitamin C is lost or destroyed quite easily. Prolonged cooking and exposure to the atmosphere quickly reduces vitamin C in foods. Slicing, reheating and adding baking soda also contribute to its destruction.

Many claims have been made about vitamin C. Some are founded and more are yet to be proven. Heavily processed dog foods have driven out the water soluble vitamin C. Combine this with the particular environment that our dogs live in today and I believe that adding vitamin C to the canine diet is something to consider.

To conclude this section on vitamins I would like to offer my own observations on vitamin supplementation. There is no doubt that the dog requires vitamins, some more than others, as we have discussed. The question then arises: is my dog getting all the vitamins he needs? We have been told by human nutritionists that if we eat a balanced diet with the proper amounts of fresh foods, we do not require vitamin supplements. Yet we take vitamins ourselves and see other people doing the same. We have been told either by our veterinarian or dog food manufacturers that if our dog eats such and such balanced, complete dog food, extra vitamin supplementation is not necessary. Why do dogs then respond to fresh foods and vitamin supplements?

I have observed many times a dramatic change in dogs fed additional vitamins and minerals that were already on well known high quality dog food. I have seen dogs, particularly older dogs, change dramatically between visits to the veterinary clinic to the point that I didn't recognize them. These individuals were coming in with ailments ranging from persistent coughs to rough, shaggy hair coats, and once put onto vitamin supplementation improved dramatically.

Most dogs today do not get fresh food but rather processed and preserved foods, in which the vitamins may have been destroyed or made unavailable to the dog.

All dogs are individuals in different environments which greatly affect their requirements. We are the best judges of whether our dog is receiving his requirements. We are told to "listen to your body" when referring to ourselves; we must do the same with our dog. Observe his body and he will tell us when he is deficient. We only have to be smart enough to read the signs. If we suspect a deficiency, a look at the diet and a trip to the veterinarian or animal nutritionist may be in order.

MINERALS

Minerals are inorganic substances found in the atmosphere and on the earth's crust. Some of these elements are found in animal tissues, and many are considered essential to life, as animals can not live without them. Minerals do not yield energy to the dog but are necessary for life so must be included as essential nutrients.

The four elements: oxygen, hydrogen, nitrogen and carbon are required by the dog, as with all of us, and are present in the air we breath and the foods we eat. These we take for granted, since they are present in tissue and are required by all living beings.

For our purposes, we shall discuss those minerals that are present in animal tissue in lesser amounts than the first four. Minerals are classified as essential which means that if they are excluded from the diet, problems will result and if supplied, the problem is corrected. Scientists have named nineteen such minerals. Another eight they have called beneficial, meaning that life is possible without them. As well, there are another twenty or thirty elements that are found in tissues, and these have been called contaminants by some experts. With further scientific research, we are going to hear more in the future about minerals. We shall deal with the major essential minerals, commonly called macrominerals, and trace elements.

The macrominerals: calcium, phosphorus, magnesium, potassium, sodium and chlorine are required in relatively large amounts every day by the dog. These minerals are involved in the structure of bones and cells and in body metabolism. Often they work in harmony with other elements or nutrients to perform a specific body function.

We must be aware of the harmony that exists in the dog's body with the many complex interactions of all nutrients playing in tune to the same symphony.

The trace elements: iron, zinc, copper, manganese, iodine, chromium, selenium, molybdenum, cobalt and sulfur are required in very small amounts by comparison and have important roles in metabolism. Others, like silicon, nickel, and florine may be put into this list as science improves the means to measure them and their benefits can be documented.

Generally, the requirements for the minerals are estimates. These estimates have been established from experimental feeding trials done with dogs and other species. Certain states such as growth, lactation and muscular effort increase the demand for minerals. Put another way, as energy requirements increase, so do mineral requirements.

Minerals also interact with each other, which can be good or bad. Essential minerals can interact with toxic elements which may lead to problems. Excesses of other nutrients such as some vitamins and amino acids may lead to deficiencies. For example, an excess of vitamin C may lead to a copper deficiency.

Because minerals are required in such small amounts, with roles that are quite subtle, deficiencies may take a long time to be noticed. With new and improved testing methods many of these can be detected early.

We know a lot about minerals. As with vitamins, however, there is still a lot to learn. We are going to discuss each of the minerals separately, briefly describing what each does, what deficiency signs may appear and what food sources provide them.

Calcium

Calcium is one of the macrominerals required by the dog, primarily for bones and teeth. Lesser amounts are used in the body fluids and for muscle and nerve function. Calcium is also important in the regulation of blood and milk formation. In the dog's body calcium, phosphorus, and vitamin D are closely related and must be considered together.

Of particular importance is the ratio between calcium and phosphorus which should be around 1.2 -1.4 parts calcium to one part phosphorus. If this ratio in the diet is not maintained, the availability of either one can change. This happens by one tying up or binding the other, resulting in the dog not getting the correct amount.

Many things can affect the calcium status of the dog besides the ratio to phophorus. Certain foods and hormones can also make a difference. Foods such as bran and unleavened bread contain substances called phytates that can bind calcium and make it unabsorbable. A high fat diet also can reduce the availability of calcium, which is an important consideration in a working dog's diet. A high protein diet will increase the loss of calcium through an acid urine as well. Hormone changes, such as spaying, eliminate estrogen production, which tends to make the bones lose calcium causing them to be weaker and more prone to fractures, much the same as in post-menopausal women.

Many things can affect the calcium status; however, one should not start supplementing "willy-nilly" as this can make things worse. If you suspect a calcium deficiency, as with any deficiency we have discussed previously, take your concerns to your dog's veterinarian so that the problem can be corrected.

Good food sources of calcium are milk, cheese, canned salmon and bone meal. Remember the adult dog may not be able to digest milk or cheese, so consider yogurt instead. Dogs of old and the wild dogs of today consumed the bones of their prey which adequately supplied all their calcium requirements. Today we are told not to feed bones because the fragments may cause problems, which is true. Our modern dogs do not have the benefit of eating hair and feathers that would protect the stomach and intestines from the sharp edges. The fiber that we feed our dogs today might not be able to replace this protection that the hair and feathers provided. Large bones that are not too brittle are acceptable in my opinion. Small fine bones such as from fish and some sharp chicken bones should be avoided.

Signs of calcium deficiency are often combined with a phosphorus and vitamin D imbalance. The earliest signs are those of osteoporosis, (porous bone, "bone softening") in the jawbones, skull bones, ribs and finally the long leg bones. Teeth may detach, gums may receed, joints can become painful and limbs may easily fracture. Young dogs may exhibit bowing of the legs (rickets), slow growth and a poor appetite.

Excess calcium can lead to kidney failure, constipation, abdominal pain and deposition of calcium in sites outside bone. Calcium is an important mineral in combination with phosphorus and vitamin D. Supplementing must be done with care, and it is advisable to get professional advice in this regard.

Puppies of the giant breeds, for example, St. Bernards and Great Danes, may require calcium, phosphorus and vitamin D supplementation, and this should be done with everything being considered. Factors such as the stage of growth, amount of mother's milk, exercise, environment and total diet composition must be considered so that the requirements are met to ensure optimal growth without imbalances from excesses.

Phosphorus

Phosphorus is closely related to calcium in both nutrition and metabolism. Like calcium, phosphorus is involved in the formation of bones and teeth and is necessary for the working of every cell in the dog's body. Magnesium and the B vitamins are also interrelated with phosphorus function.

Food sources are milk, bonemeal, poultry, meats, eggs, fish and legumes. Deficiencies appear as those of a calcium imbalance but can also lower the dog's resistance to infection, because phosphorus is involved with the immune system and white blood cell performance. Low phosphorus has also been observed to lower reproductive performance in animals. As has been said before, calcium, vitamin D and phosphorus work together and any deficiency or excess of any one of them will produce similar signs.

Magnesium

Magnesium is abundant inside cells and is closely linked with calcium and phosphorus metabolism. Most of the magnesium is found in the teeth and bones of the dog. The rest is found mainly in the cells. Magnesium is essential for the movement of sodium, potassium and calcium in and out of the cells. All are involved in maintaining the internal environment of the dog's body, so that all body functions work in harmony.

Deficiencies may result in loss of appetite, weight loss, and muscle weakness especially in the hind legs.

Food sources are bone meal, whole grains, green vegetables, nuts and shrimp. Supplementation should be done with professional guidance because of the involvement of calcium and phosphorus.

Potassium

Potassium has received a lot of attention in human nutrition of late because of its relationship in high blood pressure. Presently most reputable commercial dog foods have adequate amounts, but if a dog is on prolonged medications, such as diuretics, potassium supplementation may be required. Dogs on low potassium diets have exhibited poor growth, restlessness, muscular paralysis, tendency to dehydrate and abnormalities of the heart and kidneys.

Potassium is present in every cell of the dog's body and is required for the correct working of the heart, muscles and nervous system. It does this in conjunction with sodium, and the ratio of these two is important for the functioning of all cells. Fresh fruits, vegetables and whole grains are rich in potassium.

Sodium and Chlorine

These two minerals, or common salt, are considered together. Sodium is essential for the maintenance of the dog's body fluids and blood pressure. Working with potassium the correct fluid environment of the cells is maintained so that the cells can function. Dogs on a high meat diet will obtain their sodium from meat; however, as we feed more vegetable type foods, which are low in sodium, some salt is added. Sodium is lost through sweat or perspiration.

Dogs do not sweat or perspire much as compared to humans, so they do not lose the same amounts of sodium that we do. Sweat contains large amounts of salt, hence its salty taste. Because dogs do not lose much salt, even in warm weather, salt is not as important an ingredient in their diets as it is for us. In developing recipes for the dog, salt is often excluded.

Signs of deficiency are fatigue, retarded growth, dry skin, and loss of hair.

Iron

Iron plays a main role as an oxygen transporter in red blood cells and muscle. Its other role is in the composition of some enzymes. Wild dogs obtain most of their iron from the flesh and bones that they consume. Deficiencies will result in anemia symptoms, such as listlessness, fatigue and poor growth in puppies. Growing puppies and pregnant individuals require more iron. Foods rich in iron are red meats, liver and egg yolks. Vegetables are poor sources of iron and over boiling vegetables can reduce their iron content by as much as twenty percent. Whole grains inhibit iron absorption while vitamin C improves absorption.

Zinc

In the past few years, zinc has been given a lot of attention in human nutrition and is now thought to be an important nutrient. Zinc deficiency in dogs has been known for some time to be the cause of hair loss, thickening of the skin, disturbances in growth and poor appetite. Other conditions include delayed sexual maturity, immune deficiencies and poor wound healing.

Best food sources are mussel meats, oysters, liver, egg yolk, split peas, garlic, peanuts, whole wheat and lima beans. The availability of zinc is influenced by iron, manganese, selenium and copper, and excesses of zinc can disturb these as well. Refining and processing foods has been shown to reduce their zinc content.

If a zinc deficiency is suspected, supplementation can be tried. Reasonable amounts have not been shown to be harmful, and if the condition improves zinc may have been the problem. With the extensive studies in human nutrition, we shall hear more.

Copper

Copper is another of the essential trace minerals. It is involved with iron and the blood's ability to carry oxygen. Copper is also contained in a number of enzymes, especially those involved with brain metabolism. Deficiencies produce anemia, skeletal defects, reproductive failure and impaired immunity. Food sources include oysters, kidney, and liver. Copper has been associated for years with heart disease and arthritis in people. Some people obtain relief by wearing a copper bracelet or from copper supplementation.

Vanadium

Vanadium is considered to be of value in preventing heart disease and cancer in man. Many human vitamin-mineral supplements contain vanadium today, so we may hear more in the future with regards to the dog.

Silicon

Silicon appears to be an essential element. Silicon is similar to carbon but much stronger in chemical bonds and appears in the structural material of cartilage, tendons, skin, arteries, and cornea of the eyes.

Molybdenum

Refining foods reduces its molybdenum content, so we may see more deficiencies in the dog. It and copper interact together, so copper deficiencies may involve molybdenum.

Chromium

Chromium is an essential trace element and is necessary in blood sugar control. It has been shown to be important for the action of insulin and the regulation of normal blood sugar levels. Deficiency signs appear as clouding of the cornea of the eyes, sugar in the urine, and elevated blood sugar. The best food source is brewer's yeast.

Manganese

Manganese is found in bone, soft tissues, liver and kidney and is necessary for growth of the uterus in the female. Deficiencies may lead to disc and joint problems, birth defects, reduced fertility and poor growth. Leafy green vegetables, whole grains and tea are rich sources of manganese.

Selenium

Selenium has long been known to be essential in animal nutrition. Vitamin E and selenium are involved in muscle growth. Dandruff and ringworm have been effectively treated with selenium shampoos, so selenium appears to be essential for skin and hair tissue. Good food sources are grains grown on soil containing selenium. Excesses have been observed in livestock on soils containing high levels of selenium or from industrial wastes. Symptoms of selenium deficiency include hair loss, brittle hooves, tooth decay, poor appetite and weight loss.

Nickel

Nickel is involved in glucose metabolism and may affect insulin's effectiveness on blood sugar. It is being evaluated in people with reference to heart attacks, strokes and allergies. We may hear more later of the value of nickel in canine nutrition.

Iodine

Dogs require small amounts of iodine for the prevention of goiter. Goiter is the enlargement of the thyroid gland situated in the neck. It is instrumental in the regulation of growth so as iodine becomes deficient, the gland enlarges to compensate. Poor growth, skeletal deformities, delayed shedding of deciduous teeth, hairlessness, dullness and drowsiness can all be signs of lack of iodine. Food sources are iodized salt and kelp.

Cobalt

Cobalt is an essential trace element closely associated with vitamin B_{12}. It is required for healthy blood, in particular hemoglobin, the oxygen carrier in blood. Cobalt is required for the production of vitamin B_{12}, so a deficiency of either one may lead to anemia and listlessness. Liver, organ meats, eggs and dairy products are good sources of cobalt.

Sulfur

Although sulfur is present in all living matter and essential for life, little is known about deficiencies. It is present in all proteins and especially in the two amino acids, methione and cysteine. It is also present in some enzymes and vitamins. Since these amino acids cannot be made in the dog's body, it is believed that the sulfur is obtained primarily from the foods of animal sources. Some plants, like onions and cabbage, contain sulfur as well. If a dog is on an adequate protein diet, sulfur is not a concern.

Fluorine

Fluorine, or Fluoride, has received much publicity in human medicine for its ability to reduce tooth decay. This is probably true for the dog. Excess Fluorine has been shown to cause mottling of the tooth enamel in the dog.

To summarize this section on minerals, we have discussed those minerals that modern science considers to be essential to life. Actual requirements for most minerals have been studied, documented and symptoms of deficiencies identified. Dogs in the wild have survived for millions of years in their particular environment with their particular diet. The modern dog of today has a different environment and a different diet, so mineral supplementation has become important.

Ideally the diet should be the source of vitamins and minerals but with current means of processing, refining, and preserving foods, questions concerning mineral losses and availability are being asked.

The decision whether to supplement minerals has many considerations, one of which is the diet. Other concerns are age, sex, drug therapy, exercise, hormone status (spayed or neutered) and local environment. If a mineral deficiency is suspected, the individual dog, his diet, and his environment must be evaluated by professional people trained in the areas of health and nutrition. The whole picture must be evaluated before a diagnosis is made and corrections initiated. Hit and miss supplementing with minerals may do more harm than good. The purpose of this section is to help make the dog owner aware of what is known with regards to minerals as nutrients and appreciate that it is not a simple black and white issue.

For all practical purposes, a well-prepared commercial dog food or a diversified home prepared feeding plan with variety and fresh ingredients should provide all necessary minerals. Exceptions, as we discussed, would be calcium and phosphorus which may be needed for large, fast-growing puppies.

Now, and in the future, I believe there is a place for most individual dogs to be given a multiple vitamin-mineral supplement. This is especially true for today's active dog.

Because of our technological age, we have used some minerals for purposes that make our lives more convenient. Some of these metals have concentrated to such an extent in our environment that they have become toxic or poisonous. In particular, lead, aluminum, mercury and cadmium have become elements of concern. These metals were always present in our environment but with certain industrial and household use they have concentrated and are now causing problems for life. This is of concern to us and our pets. We live longer than our pets, allowing a greater time for these elements to concentrate in our body, but our pets are smaller in size so they can tolerate less. Our pets live in the same environment with us, so it is appropriate to briefly discuss these elements.

Lead

Lead has been known to cause stillbirths, learning problems, cancer, heart disease, depression, immune problems and death. It is in our environment from gasoline exhaust, lead-based paint to dust and dirt. In the body, lead interferes with other trace elements, for example, zinc, which can become deficient. Nutritionally, we can help reduce some of the effects by feeding foods rich in vitamins C, D, E and selenium, zinc, calcium, iron, magnesium and other nutrients.

Aluminum

Aluminum seems to affect the central nervous system and bone metabolism with possible links to Alzheimer's disease in man. Sources include aluminum cookware, processed cheeses, table salt, white flour and tap water. We may be hearing more about the affects in dogs in the future.

Mercury and Cadmium

Both of these are in our environment. Mercury can concentrate in the foods that we feed our dog and cadmium is quite high in cigarette smoke. Mercury affects the central nervous system and cadmium binds zinc.

RECOMMENDATIONS

Up until this point we have discussed the science of nutrition; now it is time to apply the art of nutrition. Like many things, the feeding and care of animals is an art as well as a science. The "green thumb" in gardening, the "management in the feed bucket" are phrases used to describe the art of gardening and that of livestock management. This known quality that combines the knowledge of the science applied to the daily application, we call art.

We can dissect and analyze to great lengths, but the bottom line is the application of this knowledge in the everyday feeding of our dog. From feeding trials in controlled environments, to computer calculations of balanced rations, it still comes down to the "eye of the beholder". Each dog is an individual with his or her particular needs in his or her particular situation. We must beware of all needs and then feed or act accordingly.

Modern science has discovered and identified many nutrients. Science has also given us some insight into which ones are required and some recommendations on how much of these nutrients should be adequate. We must realize that nutrition is a changing science and what is advisable today may not be tomorrow.

From various books and lists of tables, we can obtain nutrient recommendations. These are established for the average dog in an average situation, but in reality, there may not be such an individual. Studies are continually being done in the science of nutrition looking into the interactions of different foods, the complexities of digestion, the mechanisms of absorption and the final utilization of nutrients. All this is being done for a dog that is in a different world from what his ancestors knew.

Having said this, we must carry on with the knowledge we have now with regard to feeding our dog but be willing to be flexible as new information becomes available. If we get in trouble, we can always look back in history and ask ourselves what did the dogs of old or those in the wild do to survive? This is one of the reasons we have discussed the dog's make up and tried to relate it to his diet. We have also compared him to herbivores to illustrate the differences in body structure and diet.

The question now must be asked. How do we combine the science of nutrition with the art of feeding? To answer this question, we must first know what is normal for our dog. By recognizing the normal healthy dog, we can then go on to identify what is abnormal. For example, is it normal for my dog to have a cold wet nose, vomit occasionally, shed hair during certain times of the year, or have diarrhea after eating ice cream? The answers to all are yes; these are signs of a normal healthy dog. However, there are many signs that can tell us that our dog is not normal and, in fact, may have a problem.

Signs of Good Health:

alertness and vigor;
good appetite and regular stools;
proper weight and unblemished skin;
sturdy, well developed bones and teeth;
full, thick, and glossy haircoat;
and bright eager eyes.

If our dog has all of these signs, we are comfortable that all is well. If not, we become concerned and should either take him to the veterinarian, change his environment or take a look at his diet. The cause of the abnormality could be medical, genetic, behavioral or nutritional.

Signs of Ill-health:

irritability, listlessness, depression, hyperactivity;
aggressive, incessant crying, biting, lashing out;
poor appetite, fussiness, bad breath;
diarrhea, constipation, foul smelling stools;
obesity, thinness, puffiness, softness;
dull, dry, greasy, smelly haircoat;
red, pale, dry, flaky, itchy skin;
dull, tearing and inflamed eyes.

All of these signs could be due to improper nutrition. We are told to "listen to our body" and it will tell us if everything is fine. The same is true for our pets. Observe and they will tell us if something is wrong.

The dog will eat foods that smell right, are palatable, have a favorable texture and are free of harmful products that he finds offensive. Generally, cats like their food fresh, whereas the dog doesn't mind it aged. How often have we seen our dog bury some of his food to be dug up and enjoyed at a later date. We must listen to what he is telling us and then give him what he needs.

Let us go back over the six basic nutrients that we have discussed previously and make some general recommendations. Now the art comes in as we watch and maintain our pet in a state of good health. If we see that this state may be slipping, we adjust our feeding program accordingly, just like the "green thumb" gardener or the "bucket management" livestock farmer.

The nutrient requirements for a dog are fixed for his situation. The amount of food needed to meet these requirements will vary greatly depending on the amount of each nutrient present in the type of food eaten. In other words, providing nutritious foods containing the required nutrients is our goal.

Water is required in the largest amount of all nutrients and should be available at all times. An exception might be puppies who may tend to gulp too much water. They should be offered water periodically, rather than free access. This can be done during house training by first offering the water, then taking them outdoors soon after so that they can urinate. Utilizing the puppy's natural urge to urinate shortly after drinking may help train him in the unnatural habit we call "house training".

The dish for water should be easy to clean and resistant to wear and chewing. I personally think that cool, clean water tastes better from a metal dish than a plastic one. The type of dish will depend upon the length of your dog's ears and the shape of his face. A shallow dish is good for a puppy and the flat faced, short nose dog. A deep bowl is better for the long nose dog, and steep-sided bowls for dogs with long ears.

We do not worry about giving our dog enough water by having it available at all times, but we should become concerned if he seems to be spending a lot of time drinking and urinating. This sign may indicate that he is sick and should have a check up. Things like kidney problems, diabetes, and fever from infection are the first things that may come to mind.

Remember that dogs on a dry dog food, in warm weather, or with plentiful exercise require more water, and the safest thing is to have a dish of clean fresh water available at all times. The growing puppy and the idle adult will drink about two to three times as much water as the amount of dry matter food that they eat. A dog in hot weather, after severe exertion or lactating may drink four or more times the amount of water compared to the amount of dry matter food consumed. The best solution may be a self-regulated supply with free choice access, but cold water after extensive exercise should be avoided as water intoxication can be fatal.

Carbohydrates

We have learned that the dog requires energy and that the ancestral dog obtained this primarily from proteins and fats. We have also learned that much of this energy can be provided to the modern dog by feeding him partly processed carbohydrates. By feeding carbohydrate type foods such as the cereal grains and vegetables, we can dilute the protein down in a high meat diet. We can also lower the caloric density, (number of calories within a food) of diets containing a lot of fat. On the other hand, by adding carbohydrates, we increase the volume or bulk of the diet.

How much carbohydrate we can feed a dog will depend upon the amount of protein and fat he requires in his diet first. After these requirements are met, then the rest of his energy needs can be made up with carbohydrates. That is usually about fifty percent of the total diet.

Carbohydrate can also provide bulk and fiber to the diet and is much cheaper than proteins and fats. We must always remember to either cook, bake or grind grains and vegetables, so that the dog's digestive system can take advantages of these foods,

Carbohydrates are primarily found in cereal grains, vegetables, and fruits. These are the sugars and starches we discussed earlier. The dog, because of his small digestive system, must not be overloaded with too much bulk from carbohydrates. The wild dog consumes the stomach and intestinal contents of his prey, which would be predominately carbohydrates, so we really haven't changed our modern dog's diet much if we feed him processed carbohydrates.

Proteins are the building blocks in foods used for constructing and repairing the dog's many cells. Protein must be of good quality so that the essential amino acids are included to allow these important processes to take place in the dog. Excess protein cannot be stored as protein but is stored as fat, never to be converted back to protein. Therefore, protein must always be present in the diet. High quality protein foods come primarily from animal sources. Protein is required in greater amounts by the growing puppy, stressed individuals like the working dog and the pregnant and nursing mother dog. Lesser amounts are required for the adult and older dog.

An average daily intake of from twenty to twenty-five percent of a good quality protein will adequately provide the dog with his or her requirements, the low end for the adults and the higher percentage for puppies and stressed individuals.

The percentage of protein required in the diet will vary with

- digestibility (animal protein is easier to digest than plant sources)
- the amino acid composition (especially the essentials)
- the caloric density of the diet (more fat, more protein)
- the physiological state of the dog (puppy, adult, etc.)

Inadequate quality protein in the dog's diet will appear as poor growth, rough haircoat, anemia, listlessness, a drop in milk production, weight loss, and susceptibility to infections and toxins from the environment.

We must always be thinking about protein when we feed our dog. He must have it to stay in good health. Excess can be expensive as protein foods are costly, and the protein not used for building and repair will be used for energy or stored as fat. In other words, we can supply energy with less expensive foods such as carbohydrates, so feeding excess protein is pointless.

Fats

Nature's powerful energy food, fats, not only provide over twice the amount of energy fuel of proteins and carbohydrates; they also contain the tasty flavors that dogs enjoy. Just because they taste good, however, is no reason to allow the dog to over indulge.

Because of their acceptable flavor, fats can be used to enhance the palatability of a meal. We must remember to reduce the other energy foods like carbohydrates, for if we continue with a high calorie diet the dog may become overweight.

Fats are required as an essential nutrient for cell structure and vitamin sources so must always be present in the diet. Recommendations vary from five percent of the diet to more with higher levels not a concern if adequate protein is also available. Generally, the more fat in the diet, the more protein as well. Coarse dry hair and flaking of the skin are the first signs a dog will show when the essential fatty acids are deficient.

Vitamins and Minerals

These subtle essential nutrients play many different roles in the dog's well-being and good health. Vitamin and mineral supplementing has received much attention lately with the human popularity of this subject. As far as the dog is concerned, a multi vitamin-mineral supplement may be in order if our dog is suspect of a deficiency. Dogs eating only one commercial brand of dogfood with no variety or fresh foods, have, in my experience, benefited from supplementation. As well, dogs that are given only one particular food are subject to vitamin and mineral deficiencies. Over supplementing, especially with fat soluble vitamins and minerals, can be dangerous and should only be done under professional guidance.

PART TWO Commercially Prepared Dog Food

MOST PET OWNERS
Don't
have much knowledge of nutrition,
have much experience feeding animals,
have access to cheap supplies of dog food,
and
don't have the time or desire to cook for the pet
so
they depend on reliable prepared pet foods.

The Pet Food Industry is a young industry that has grown rapidly into a multi-billion dollar business. Walk into any supermarket and see the huge selection of pet foods available. Pet foods of every variety and price are at our disposal. From this huge selection, we attempt to read labels and pick what we think our pet might like from the name and pictures on the containers. Struggling with our subconscious over media ads and always watching our budget, we make our selection.

We have become vulnerable to the market and the media. Are we really wise and informed shoppers when we pick a dogfood to take home? With today's technology and knowledge of nutrition, we would have to spend a lot of time studying to stay current. The average pet owner has been left behind in the rush. We must rely on others for guidance. Armed, however, with some basic knowledge, we can be informed and wise consumers.

In this rush of technology, the public must be protected, so governments make laws to protect us. Laws have been enacted which apply to the manufacturing and sales of pet food products, including ingredients, labeling and storage. Often, the laws are made and enforced after an industry is in mass production.

In Part I, "Nutrition and Nutrients", we covered the basics of dog nutrition including digestion and absorption. Then we went over the six nutrient groups, discussing each nutrient, what it does, where it is found and what can happen if it is missing.

In Part II, we shall take a look at commercially prepared dog foods. This very young industry saw the demand and is supplying products that are selling in the billions of dollars today. We shall list the various uses and kinds of dogfood on the market today, discussing the advantages and disadvantages of each, outlining how to shop for these products and listing guidelines on how to feed them when we get home.

As consumers purchasing these products we must

- know what our pet requires;
- select a prepared pet food product that supplies the requirements in the adequate proportions;
- stay within our budget;
- evaluate the product after our pet has eaten it; and
- make adjustments when necessary.

Companies involved in the Pet Food Industry have spent much time and money, some more than others, on research and development of pet foods. Using this research, they are manufacturing and selling pet foods that should be supplying the necessary nutritional requirements from the various ingredients used. Some say these ingredients are really, "left-overs or table scraps" of the people food industry. It is up to us as consumers to evaluate the products and understand what we are buying. These "left-overs" or by-products may become the ingredients for the dog food we buy. Some companies may not use this type of ingredient but the raw primary product instead. This costs more to produce; therefore, the company must charge more for its final product. The less expensive dog foods that rely on by-products for their ingredients will vary between batches as price and availability of this type of ingredient fluctuates. The old adage, "you get what you pay for," applies to dog food as well.

DOG FOOD: YESTERDAY, TODAY AND TOMORROW

Millions of years ago, dogs hunted for their food just like wild carnivores do today. As dogs were domesticated by man, we fed them what we were eating. It was not until the late 1800's that the first commercial dog food was made. In the 1860's, an American, James Spratt, was making and selling Spratt's Dog Cake in England, which was a mixture of wheat meal, beetroot, meat and vegetables.

The first dog foods were baked biscuits made from grains. Biscuits could be stored and transported easily without losing food value, and, when combined with fresh meat, made adequate pet food. Later dog meal appeared, a by-product of the human breakfast industry. Many companies are still making both today. Dried meat was incorporated with the cereal grain meals to make a more complete dog food. Human and dog food processing evolved during this same period with the goal being convenience for the consumer.

In order for food to be prepared and kept for long periods of time, the science of food preservation had to be expanded beyond the common means of the day: salting, drying, and freezing. Canning developed in the mid 1800's, making canned meat available for people. It was from this industry of canning meat for human consumption that the canning of dog food developed using the less desirable portions. During this time, a Canadian veterinarian, Dr. Ballard, was canning a home made product of his own. His is a household name today.

Canning of dog food lead to sales. This was convenient. Consumers bought and by the 1930's, nearly two hundred brands of dog food were available for pet owners. Companies conducted research and feeding trials to make their products nutritious and tasty, and advertised accordingly.

Today, seven billion dollars is spent each year on pet food in the United States, six hundred million a year in Canada and six hundred million a year in Western Europe. It has been estimated that the sales volume of pet food today exceeds the human ready-to-eat cereal and instant breakfast food sales combined.

The pet food industry is big business today. Walk into any supermarket and you will see a whole aisle devoted entirely to pet food. There are over 150 manufacturers selling over 2000 brands, ranging from dry and canned to semi-moist dog food. Supermarkets, veterinarians, livestock feed stores and pet stores all sell dog food today.

Because this industry grew so quickly, there have been some growing pains. Regulations and standards had to be developed to catch up to the huge volumes of pet food consumed. Today, concerned groups, including food manufacturers, pet owners and veterinarians, are becoming involved. For example, the AAFCO or the Association of American Feed Control Officials in the United States is involved in regulating pet food manufacturing. The CVMA, Canadian Veterinary Medical Association, has developed guidelines for manufacturers with accreditations, for those that comply.

For example, the AAFCO defines a complete food as "*a nutritionally adequate feed for animals other than man; by specific formula is compounded to be fed as the sole ration and is capable of maintaining life and for promoting production without any additional substance being consumed except water*".

The United Kingdom Feedstuffs Regulations (1981) defines a complete feedstuff, as " *a compound feedstuff which by reason of its composition is sufficient to ensure a daily ration. A daily ration is the total quantity of feedstuff expressed on a twelve percent moisture basis, required by an animal of a given kind, age group, and level of production, in order to satisfy its average daily nutritional needs*".

The complete food concept developed as pet owners were feeding prepared products as the sole daily meal. If these products were not nutritionally adequate, deficiencies soon became evident in the pets, especially the young fast growing individuals.

Because this industry has grown so fast, there are many unanswered questions about the feeding of these products to our pets. For example, we don't know the long term effects of the preservatives and additives on our pets. Also what happens to these products when they are combined with products in the environment? An example would be the recent concern about free radicals in human medicine and nutrition. What really happens during the processing of these products to the many nutrients that we know, and what about the ones we don't know?

Questions will be answered with time. In time, Government regulations will catch up to the demands of the consumers, so that products will improve, and more precise labeling will allow us to make better buying choices.

The future for the pet food industry looks very good in that the age group of pet owners from forty-five to fifty-five years of age spend the most on pet food, and this amount is to increase fifty percent by the year 2000. As well, the possibility of new markets in other countries around the world makes the growth of the pet food industry likely.

I have some thoughts on what the pet foods of the future may be. We are going to see more information on the labels. We may see packages of dog food that we take home and mix with fresh ingredients; this will remove the need for some preservatives and additives and reduce packaging and freight costs. We will see more specialized, specific dog foods, for example, a food for urban dogs living in high pollution areas made up of anti-oxidants like vitamins E and C. As the industry evolves, all dogs will benefit.

KINDS OF DOG FOOD

There are many kinds of commercial dog food available to us today. The three common types are dry, soft-moist and canned. The most popular of these three are the dry dog foods. All have the same basic ingredients, usually grains, meat meal, vegetables, dairy products, vitamins and minerals.

Dry dog foods today are either expanded, biscuit, or kibbled. The expanded forms are made by mixing the ingredients, cooking, then whipping this into a homogeneous mass that is then pushed through a die and expanded with steam and air into nuggets. The nuggets are then dried and packaged into air tight, usually plastic lined, paper bags. The biscuits and kibble, (biscuits that have been broken up) are made by mixing the ingredients into a dough. The dough is then rolled out, cut into shapes, and baked just as we would make biscuits in our own kitchens. Dry foods have about twelve percent moisture and should be used within three months of manufacturing.

Soft-moist dog foods have a higher water content which gives them the soft texture. However, because of the high moisture content, bacteria and molds can easily grow and spoilage occur. To prevent this, preservatives and humectants are added. The common humectants, that take up water, not allowing bacteria to use it, are propylene glycol and sorbitol. The preservatives are sugars and syrups which prevent bacterial growth and add flavor and energy. Artificial coloring is added and the portions are packaged in individual cellophane wrappers to prevent spoilage. Soft moist dogfoods will have from fifteen to thirty percent moisture and a shelf life of several months.

Canned foods are sealed in tin-plated steel cans that are heated to sterilize the contents. Various ingredients are used in canned dog food, but you will note that they all have a high water, protein and fat content which may be the reason that canned dog foods are the most palatable of all the commercial products. Canned foods have about seventy-five percent moisture.

Dry, soft-moist and canned are just different ways to designate prepared and preserved dog food. Each has advantages and disadvantages that we as consumers must evaluate for our needs.

Dry foods are more economical, require no refrigeration and do not spoil after the bag is opened. Because of the hard nature of these foods, the act of chewing is beneficial to the health of the teeth and jaws of our pet. However, dry foods may not have enough fat, and the fat may become rancid with storage. Also dry foods may not be as palatable or as easily digested as the others. We must always supply drinking water. The bag may become contaminated with insects or mice, once opened. Puppies, if allowed to engorge, can bloat when the dry food expands within their little stomachs.

Soft-moist requires no refrigeration, is usually quite palatable and comes packaged in convenient portions. Disadvantages are that the contents spoil, if they get wet, and may cause digestive upsets in some dogs. We may not like our pets consuming sugar and preservatives in these amounts.

Canned foods have a long shelf life, if not opened, are usually highly palatable and are the most digestible of the three. On the other hand, this is an expensive way to preserve food, and once opened must be refrigerated. We also may not wish to pay for water, as these foods are seventy-five percent or more water. Since very little chewing is required, our pet's teeth may not remain nice and shiny.

Other categories we see when we purchase dog foods, especially dry and canned foods, are those prepared for particular situations, for example: growth rations for growing puppies, maintenance rations for adults and reducing rations for obese dogs. There are also dietary foods formulated to be fed to dogs having a specific disease, such as a low-salt diet for dogs with congestive heart failure. These are called prescription diets.

HOW TO SHOP FOR PREPARED DOG FOOD

"The proper selection of a dog food is the most important thing a dog feeder does."
  Dr. Donald R. Collins, *The Collins Guide to Dog Nutrition.*

As dog owners, we have the sole responsibility of feeding our dog. If we don't do it right, the dog will suffer because he cannot roam around the neighborhood and pick up what he may be lacking. Our dog is totally dependent upon us to supply all his nutritional needs. Purchasing the right dog food becomes an important decision. Almost all dog owners in North America have bought a manufactured dog food at one time. Why did we pick the brands that we did? I would suspect probably the following reasons:

- Cost and availability
- Palatability, will our dog eat it?
- Does our dog "smell" or have "loose" bowel movements after eating a certain brand?
- Media advertising, colorful packaging, convenience
- Advice from:
  - Breeder,
  - Kennel manager,
  - Pet store clerk,
  - Groomer,
  - Neighbor, or
  - Veterinarian.

From my experience and observations, this is how we decide which dog food to buy. Let's be wiser shoppers and select the best for our pet within our budget. Buying dog food is like buying any other food or consumer item for the home. We should inform ourselves, select what we need, make the purchase and evaluate what we bought when we get home.

To make a wise selection

- Have a basic understanding of our pet's nutritional needs;
- Read the label understanding what it says and does not say;
- Buy wisely regarding cost;
- Buy and feed our dog what he or she requires;
- Once purchased open and evaluate the package and contents;
- Test the product by feeding and observing the dog;
- Change or supplement if necessary;

With a basic understanding of nutrition, we can read labels, give table scraps, supplement with vitamins and evaluate our dogs performance. A basic understanding gives us confidence that we are doing the right thing. Canine nutrition is much the same as human and other animal nutrition, with the few exceptions that we have discussed in Part I of this book. Nutrition is not a difficult science; after all, we have been eating for many years.

Read books on nutrition and send for information from the dog food companies. Seek out nutritionists and veterinarians with an interest and knowledge in canine nutrition. Ask for their advice.

Cost is a concern for all of us. Remember, we "get what we pay for" applies to dog food like many other things we buy. Quality costs more. In dog food manufacturing, the most expensive parts are the ingredients, as compared to the packaging and processing. So if a product appears cheaper, it is probably a good bet that the ingredients were cheaper. Dog food has traditionally been made from the "table scraps" of the people food industry, commonly referred to as by-products. These products often are nutritionally adequate for the dog, but, because we would not eat them ourselves, for whatever reason, they are sold as dog food ingredients. Obviously ingredients that could be used as human food would cost more for the manufacturer.

Reading the Label

When making our selection, we must read and understand the label. By law, foods are labeled in a required format.

The label is the statement made by the manufacturer with regards to various claims. By reading the label, we, as consumers, can learn a lot. We may have to read between the lines on some things, but generally the more information on the label, the more confidence we can have in the product.

The basic information that a manufacturer is required to put on the container includes the following

- The product name (a brand name);
- Kind of pet food: Dog Food (or Cat Food) ;
- The net weight (the weight of the product less container);
- Guaranteed analysis: at least the
    minimum crude fat and crude protein and
    maximum moisture and crude fiber;
- The list of ingredients in decreasing order of amount by weight;
- A statement of nutritional capability;
- The name and address of the manufacturer or distributor.

Other label information could be the feeding directions, a caloric statement, an ingredient claim (example no soy, or all beef), a certified stamp of standards, such as the Canadian Veterinary Medical Association seal of standards, or a nutritional need like a puppy claim or specific condition (a heart or kidney diet) may also be on the label.

Dog food labels can vary from the basic legal requirements to much more. The more information provided, the better able pet owners are to evaluate the contents of the container. And we also have a good indication that the manufacturer is confident of the quality of the product and is eager to share information about it.

An example of a dog food label;

Claim	100% complete nutrition, or Puppy Food
Net weight	NET WT. 10 POUNDS
Feeding instruction	FEEDING UNIT [Approximate number of calories/day required by a 20 lb. dog] SIZE: 7 oz. [2 cups]
Calorie statement	CALORIES:..700 per feeding unit % of calories from:

Fat [20g] 24%
Carbohydrate [76g] 45%
Protein [54g] 31%

Guaranteed analysis GUARANTEED ANALYSIS: Each feeding unit contains:

Crude Protein [54g] 27%
Crude Fat [20g] 10%
Crude Fiber [10g] 5%
Ash [16g] 8%
Moisture [27g] 12%
Calcium 1.5g
Phosphorus 1.4g
Sodium 900mg
Magnesium 175mg

Ingredients INGREDIENTS: Meat and Bone Meal, Ground Yellow Corn, Wheat Middlings, Poultry Meal, Corn Gluten Meal, Animal Fat, Salt, Yeast, Calcium Carbonate, Iron Sulfate, Magnesium Oxide, Zinc Oxide, Copper Oxide, Vitamin A, D , E , B , Supplements , Calcium Pantothenate, Biotin, Thiamine Mononitrate, Riboflavin Supplement, Ethylendiamine Dihydriodide, Pyridoxine Hydrochloride, Folic Acid, Manganase Oxide, and Sodium Selenite.

This is a label on which the company is telling the consumer about its product. Everything is quite straightforward. The ingredients are listed in order of amount present, with the first on the list being the largest amount present, and so on in decreasing order. The various ingredients are listed; however, the sources are not.

What's in a label?

What does a label tell us and what doesn't it tell us?
Let's go through the seven items we listed previously and comment.

Name

The name is an important marketing concept in that it is hoped that we will first become interested in buying this particular brand. Manufacturers hope we will remember when we need to purchase more later. Some names are cute or unusual for this purpose. Other names may be used to depict a flavor such as beef or chicken, just as with people food like Italian. Specific names are sometimes used to address a particular nutritional purpose or disease condition, directing these products to individual dogs. Examples would be puppy, adult, or kidney or heart diets. "What's in a name" is important from a marketing stand point, and dog food is no exception.

Kind of pet food

The words "Dog Food" or "Cat Food" specify that one is for dogs and the other for cats, because the two are different. Dog food will not have as much fat or protein as cat food and the ingredients will differ. Cats have different protein and vitamin requirements, so the formulation is not the same.

Net Weight

The net weight number tells us the weight of the contents. This figure we can use to comparison shop. By dividing the cost by the net weight, we have a price per pound or ounce, kilogram or gram. Just because the containers may be the same size, does not mean that the contents are the same. Something else to consider is the moisture content; more water means less dry matter, which contains the nutrients.

This required statement by the manufacturer lists the minimum amounts allowed for the energy nutrients of fat and protein and the maximum allowed for non-energy fiber and moisture.

This does not tell us the actual amount of the ingredient or anything about the quality but is a rough guide to the composition. The illustration may help explain how these chemical contents are determined in a process called a proximate analysis.

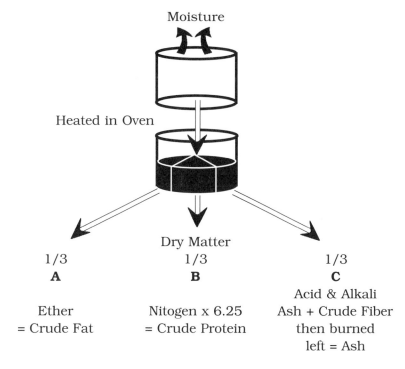

Moisture

Heated in Oven

Dry Matter

1/3	1/3	1/3
A	**B**	**C**
		Acid & Alkali
Ether	Nitogen x 6.25	Ash + Crude Fiber
= Crude Fat	= Crude Protein	then burned
		left = Ash

∴ Carbohydrate = 100% - (Fat + Protein + Ash + Fiber + Moisture)

The sample of dog food is placed in an oven and dried to remove the moisture. The remaining dry matter is divided into three equal parts. One is extracted with ether to determine crude fat, another undergoes a nitrogen analysis and the nitrogen content multiplied by 6.25 to give crude protein, and the third is processed in acid and alkali to give ash (mineral) and fiber.

Now, by adding up protein + fat + ash + fiber + moisture and subtracting from one hundred we will get the carbohydrate content.

This proximate analysis is quite accurate for the chemical content of the dog food, but it does not tell us anything about the quality of the nutrients, the digestibility or the individual vitamin, mineral or essential fatty acid content. For example, remember when we discussed protein and how protein is in many things from eggs and meat to corn and feathers. The quality of the protein is valued by its contents of essential amino acids present and its digestibility.

We should look for

- canned: at least 4 % fat and 0.3 % calcium and no more than 75 % water.
- dry: at least 10 % fat and 25 % protein for growth or 20 % protein for maintenance (adult)

Some manufacturers are listing ash or minerals such as calcium and phosphorus as well as vitamins.

Ingredients

The AAFCO publishes over 500 animal feed ingredient definitions, with over 200 of these used in petfoods.

Originally, canned dog food and later dry meal were the first kinds of commercial dog food available. The canned food was made primarily with meat and meat by-products cooked with barley, wheat, corn meal and some minerals. In the mid 1950's, dry petfoods were developed and the main ingredients at that time were corn, soybean meal, corn gluten meal, wheat middlings, meat and bone meal, vitamins and minerals. By the 1970's, dry dog food was outselling canned. The early problem with dry food was getting the dogs to eat it. One of the first enhancers for palatability was lypolized white tallow sprayed on the food. Flavor enhancers continued to be an important part of this business. Acceptablity is important for sales. Even though the dog food is balanced and complete, the dog must want to eat it.

New technology lead to the development of new ingredients and, in turn, to new products such as meatballs, formed meat chunks, ersatz meat chunks, soft dry foods, dual phase extruded dry and soft moist products, high protein, high meat, and high fat dry dog foods. Some of the new ingredients developed allowing the production of these products would include propylene glycol, for a humectant in soft moist food; textured vegetable proteins in ersatz meat; food starch, gums and colors in gravy products; artificial flavors and colors; BHA, BHT, ethoxyquin and mold inhibitors as preservatives of fat and flours; gums and sodium and phosphorus salts for binders in meatballs. Research and development with new patents are continuing in this field.

As consumer demands influence the market place, the list of petfood ingredients will be changed; some new ones will be added and others will be dropped.

Each ingredient used in making the dog food is listed in descending order by weight, with the most listed first, and the least listed last. Only AAFCO approved ingredient names are used. This can be misleading in several ways.

- Cereal grains may be listed several different times; for example, ground corn, kibbled corn, flaked corn etc. which in reality is all corn and if called such might be first on the list.
- All-inclusive terms are not particularly descriptive. By-products, what does this mean? Poultry by-products, for example, may be everything from good quality necks, backs and wings or poor quality heads, feathers and feet. Cereal by-products can also vary. Instead of the whole grain, the by-products of milling such as wheat middlings, oat hulls or bran may be the ingredient.
- An ingredient may be included on the list in its dry form which is lighter than if it was weighed wet, and, therefore, can appear further down the list, for example, wheat flour vs meat or liver.

- Pet foods may have a fixed formula list that does not change according to the changing cost or supply of an ingredient. Many have an open formulation and the contents of the food may change from batch to batch, depending on the cost and availability of ingredients. This might explain why our dog may show digestive disturbances when we feed a new bag of the same brand.
- The complete composition of the food may not be listed. Preprocessed ingredients are used and their ingredients may not be on the label, for example, antioxidants present in the sources of fat such as animal fat or animal by-products.
- Terms like natural, organic, low fat and high fiber really must be uniformly defined so that we can buy accordingly.

We should look for

- canned or soft moist food: an animal source protein in the first two ingredients and at least one cereal with a source of calcium (example, bone, chicken, or fishmeal). High meat diets may be calcium and phosphorus imbalanced, so calcium is added.

- dry food: an animal source protein in the first three listed ingredients.

Animal based ingredients generally have a higher quality protein with a better balance of amino acids, vitamins and minerals than plant based ingredients.

Vitamins and minerals will be on the list near the end. Additives, such as flavors and flavor enhancers, colors, emulsifiers, preservatives, humectants, anti-oxidants and antimicrobials are also on the list.

Statement of Nutritional Capability

Statements such as nutritionally adequate, complete or balanced, state that the product, when fed as the sole diet without any other food or supplement, meets or is greater than the dog's requirements. Specifically, this applies to one or more of gestation, lactation, growth, maintenance or all stages of the dog's life cycle.

These claims can be made if the food passes certain feeding tests or contains the minimum amount of each nutrient recommended by the National Research Council (NRC). The NRC is a government agency that has made statements concerning the amount of nutrients animals and people require, based on collection of research data in these areas. NRC recommendations do not tell us about digestibility, absorption or utilization of the nutrients, nor do they indicate toxins or nutrient excesses. The best claims are those that are backed up by feeding trials on fairly large numbers of dogs over an extended length of time.

Two exceptions to these claims are "snacks" or "treats" or the statement that the product should be fed under supervision of a veterinarian.

Watch for these claims and understand the limitations.

Name and Address of Manufacturer or Distributor

Use this address or telephone number to request information regarding ingredients, protein and fat digestibility, vitamins, additives, and feeding trials results. Also ask about the quality and consistency of the ingredients.

The label contains a lot of information with some reservations as we have discussed. In the future we will see more. Much can be learned from the label before we have purchased the product; once we get home the evaluation process continues.

Other things that you may see on a label could be the CVMA, Canadian Veterinary Medical Association seal of certification. This certification states that the company voluntarily asked to have its pet food certified to meet the standards of the CVMA program. This indicates that

- The products are tested by the CVMA in a third party laboratory.
- Products must prove with twelve months production that they are capable of meeting a normal pet's nutritional requirements throughout all phases of life.
- Feeding trials are done to ensure that the nutrients in the products are not only present but biologically available or digestible to the animal.
- Once a product achieves certification, it is monitored to ensure that it continuously meets CVMA's high standards for composition, digestibility and palatability.
- Only those pet foods that have met the CVMA standards display the seal of certification.

(This information is taken from *A Commonsense Guide to Feeding Your Dog and Cat*) More information about this program can be obtained from: The CVMA Pet Food Certification Program 339 Booth Street, Ottawa, Ontario K1R 7K1, (613) 236-1162

You may also see a PFAC, NAP (Pet Food Association of Canada, Nutrition Assurance Program) logo. This is a voluntary industry program, with brands participating carrying the following standardized nutritional statement: *"Animal feeding tests using procedures outlined in the PFAC Nutrition Assurance Program show that (Brand) provides complete and balanced nutrition for (Life Stage)."* Pet Food Association of Canada, 1435 Goldthorpe Road, Mississauga, Ontario L5G 3R2, (416) 891-2921

For U.S. AAFCO - see Appendix 1 page 236.

There are five main types of dog food manufactured and sold:

- Premium brands: veterinary clinics and pet stores;
- Specific Purpose brands: veterinary clinics;
- Popular brands: grocery stores;
- Private label: grocery stores, feed stores;
- Generic brands: feed stores, grocery stores.

Premium brands stress quality and performance. The ingredients used are more selective and constant; therefore, these are the most expensive to buy. The formulation is fixed. However, because of better digestibility and nutrient density, less is required per feeding. Premium brands are also offered for certain life stages such as Growth, Active, Inactive, Lactation, or Reducing. Because of this variation in products offered, premium brands are sold through veterinary clinics or pet stores where some direction can be given to the buyers.

Specific Purpose Brands are primarily prescription type diets. The food is formulated for individual dogs with a specific need or for the elimination of a particular nutrient or nutrients. Examples are

- restricted protein for kidney disease and failure;
- bland, low fiber for gastro-intestinal upsets;
- low calorie, high fiber for obesity and reducing;
- lamb and rice for intolerance and food allergies;
- low salt for congestive heart failure;
- low mineral, restricted protein for bladder stones;
- high protein, high energy for growth and convalescing.

Some foods may be medicated, for example, with wormer or an oral contraceptive for females. The list can go on and on as consumer demands are met for the various types of diets.

Popular brands are the dog foods that will be advertised in the popular media and sold primarily in grocery stores. The formulations are usually varied, and a list of possible ingredients that could be used is printed on the label. Variable formulas allow the manufacturer to use those ingredients that are available at the time of manufacture. Popular brands are formulated and targeted at the maintenance level of nutritional requirement. With these popular brands, palatability, packaging and advertising are stressed more than optimal nutrition.

Private Label dog foods are manufactured by one company, then packaged for another company which will sell it. The label will state this. The manufacturer's name may not be present, only the name of the distributor. Here the prime concern is cost. If a manufacturer can purchase cheap ingredients and make up a dog food for less than its competitors, it will get the tender to package for the distributor. These products are less expensive.

The generic dog foods are those that are usually produced and marketed locally. They are the cheapest. Private label and generic dog foods are usually manufactured by the same company. They may have a local brand name or "no-name". These products are made with the least expensive ingredients available at the time and may or may not have considered the nutritional aspects, other than to have the minimum allowed. The big selling feature here is cost. As we have said before, "we get what we pay for". Poor quality foods, fed over any length of time, may be harmful and make supplementing necessary.

The various types of dog foods all have their place. They all have their advantages and disadvantages. Become a wise consumer and understand what you are purchasing and remember - "buyer beware".

Now that we have bought the dogfood, we start to evaluate it.

Cost

A simple calculation can be done to find out what it costs to feed our dog everyday. When we get home, we should write down the date and price of the dog food. We feed the dog food as we always do until it is all gone and note the date. Now we add up how many days our dog took to eat it and divide the number of days into the price we paid. This is the cost of the dog food per day. If we would like to calculate home recipes costs, we can keep track of the ingredients and their prices. We add this to the price we paid for the commercial dog food before we divide it by the number of days.

Now we have an idea of how much money we are spending per day to feed our dog. We may find that keeping our dog in good condition can be done quite reasonably with good quality commercial dog food. We may not have to feed as much per day as we would if we relied on a cheaper lower quality brand.

$$\frac{\text{cost of the dog food}}{\text{days of feeding in bag}} = \text{cost per day}$$

The amount fed per day becomes the critical factor. Another calculation you may want to try is to calculate the cost per day of calories fed. Some labels may have the number of calories per cup. We can calculate the cost from this approach. Either method is a useful exercise in helping us make our decisions for purchase. Calories are energy. The most expensive ingredients are proteins and fats.

Containers and Contents

Before we open the bag, can or box we should look at the container more closely and beware of tears, stains (fat stains from inside) or dents in cans. We might, if we have a fairly accurate scale, weigh the bag or can. Remember, the net contents is the weight of the contents less the container.

If we suspect something is amiss, either with the proclaimed weight or contents, we can ask the provincial, federal or state consumers affairs people to have a look at the product. Dog foods are under their jurisdiction. So, if we doubt that the product meets the label statements for ingredients, nutritional claims, moisture content or weight, it is our duty to bring this to the attention of the company and the governing authorities.

Many manufacturers list a toll-free number and a code on the container which identifies where and when it was packaged. If calling, be prepared to quote this code and keep some of the contents in case they or the Government people would like to examine it.

Open the bag. Examine the layers of the bag; a multi-layered bag of paper and plastic is preferred to wax paper. The layers are to keep moisture and aroma in, prolonging freshness. The multi-layers add strength to the bag for shipping, as well as keeping out insects and mice.

Smell the contents of the bag and evaluate the consistency. We might want to try a little test of our own. Take some of the food and heat it in a sauce pan with a little water. If the smell is offensive or off, maybe another brand should be considered next time. Beware of foreign materials or "moving creatures", all signs of poor quality. Mold also can develop, giving the food a musty smell, and maybe a white or black dusty coating to the food. Few crumbs should remain once the bag is empty.

With canned food, check for sour, rancid or off odors, but don't be concerned with the dark hole, the result of the air pocket created during canning. Cut through the food and spread it out on a plate, so you can observe the contents. Try to identify the contents. Look for undesirable contents such as hair, feathers, sharp pieces of bone, or anything that doesn't look like grain or identifiable muscle, tendon, or desirable animal by-products.

When buying soft-moist foods, check the package. Any tears or breaks in the wrapping can dry out and contaminate the food. Again, beware of unusual odors or colors. This type of food should be spongy but not feel wet. If there is any doubt, the product should be returned for a refund.

These are all things that we can do before we give the food to our dog. If something is not right we should return the dog food. There is a caution that we have for commercial products. They often are processed some time before purchase, and one doesn't know what may have happened during shipping and storage. If the package, be it either bag, box, or can is damaged in any way, beware, as the contents can be altered, and serious problems may arise if the food is to be eaten. An example of contamination of canned food is botulism. This is a deadly bacterial toxin that can be produced in air tight cans of food. Dented cans may be a warning of this contamination. When we are buying dogfood, we should take time to examine the package or can for tears and dents, and we should stay away from bargain discounts on old or damaged commercial dog food.

If we are satisfied with our visual inspection, it is time for the ultimate test. Feed our dog. This is the only way to test palatability, protein, fat, vitamin, mineral and fiber content. Some companies perform feed trials with their products, and we can obtain this information by contacting them. However, these trials may be done only on a few dogs in a controlled environment. The best is to try it on our dog at home in his or her own environment.

The Home Feeding Trial

When evaluating a particular dog food, feed only this product. Do not give anything else such as vitamin/mineral supplements or table scraps during the test as these could alter the evaluation.

To perform this evaluation, we should concentrate on three areas.

Appearance and condition of the Dog

Good	SIGNS &	Bad
	eyes	
bright, alert, clear		dull, cloudy, tearing, red
	nose	
cool, moist, clean, soft		hot, dry, hard
	teeth	
clean, white, shiny,		dirty, yellow, foul smelling
	ears	
clean, dry,		inflamed, waxy, foul smelling
	hair	
shiny, soft, clean		dull, dry, dandruff, hair loss
	skin	
soft, pliable,		dry, greasy, inflamed, itchy
	muscle	
firm, developed, defined		soft
	body condition	
can feel ribs		obese, pot belly, waddles
	paws	
smooth, resilient		cracked, sore, nails brittle
	anus	
clean, dry		inflamed, itchy anal glands
	urine	
light yellow, average volume		dark or clear, large amount

The eyes and skin are two nutritionally sensitive organs that will show signs early when deficiencies arise.

Behavior

A healthy, properly fed dog, receiving all the requirements of energy, protein, fat, vitamins, minerals and water will be happy, active and responsive. If we observe any change, we should be concerned. If the dog is irritable, dull, hyperactive, nervous or restless, the cause may be the diet. Also an increase in the consumption of water, with frequent urinations may be diet related. Any changes in behavior after we start a new diet should be noted. Usually, behavioral changes will not appear until several weeks after the dog has been on the new food.

Stools

The dog's stools are also a good indicator of the quality of the diet. A good quality diet and a properly functioning digestive system will yield a small amount of formed, dark brown, firm stools. The small amount tells us that the food has been digested, and there is little waste left. The smell will be normal. Colour can also indicate food dyes, internal bleeding and disease problems, see Liver Problems (page 216).

Stool quality and quantity can tell us a lot about the food. Water intake, fiber level, digestibility and health can be assessed from the stool.

- water intake: If not enough water is consumed, the stools will be dry, hard and difficult to pass.

- fiber level: Fiber determines the bulk of the stools. Because it is not digested, a lot of feces would indicate a lot of fiber or poor quality ingredients. Fiber is an important constituent of the dog's diet. In the wild, the dog would obtain fiber from hair, or feathers from the various prey that he had captured. Today, the manufacturer of dog food utilizes the indigestible cellulose parts of grains for fiber.

- digestibility: High quality animal-source protein, properly processed fat and carbohydrate are efficiently digested in the small intestine. The nutrients are then absorbed, leaving a small percentage of waste. Poor quality food results in undigested material passing into the large intestine where fermentation from bacteria produces gas and loose stools. This becomes evident by flatulence and diarrhea.

- health: If the dog's intestines are infected or infested with worms, the stools will be abnormal. Liver or pancreas problems will also decrease digestion and stools will not be normal.

If something is wrong with the dog's digestive system or the diet is of poor quality or contaminated, the stools may be soft, loose, watery, light-colored or black, and smelly. If this continues, the dog should be examined by your veterinarian to insure that the problem is not medical. Try to remember if the dog ate anything unusual or if something changed in his or her environment. Dogs, like people, can have food intolerances and allergies to certain foods, food additives or things in their surroundings.

From these three basic parameters: body appearance and condition, overall behavior and the stool quality and quantity, we can make a fairly accurate assessment of our dog's health and diet. Any obvious change in any of these three areas should be a concern. Some dietary deficiencies, such as a lack of a vitamin or mineral, may take a long time before the outward signs become obvious. We have the advantage of observing this because we see our dog everyday.

We should continue the evaluation for at least three weeks or more. During this test period, we make note of anything abnormal. Itching, an offensive body odor, or increased hair loss may be some of the first signs we see. Weight loss, combined with an increase in appetite with the same volume fed as before, may indicate a poorer quality dog food. The fact that we are feeding the same amount but the dog appears hungry and is losing condition could be the result of a food manufactured with poor quality ingredients with fewer digestible nutrients.

If the dog is gaining weight and is in good condition, we may find that we can decrease the amount given per day. This indicates the food is of high quality. Because less is required, the cost per day could be the same or less than the other food, even though the cost per bag was more. It is important to calculate the cost per day because this gives us a more accurate indication. In other words, if the bag costs us more but lasts longer, the cost per day will be less.

Several weeks into the test it may become evident that this food requires supplementation. Table scraps with added fat or vitamin and mineral supplements may be required. Fresh food recipes might be something to consider.

Storage

Once a container of dogfood has been opened the contents are exposed to the environment. Canned food, once opened, must be covered and refrigerated to prevent spoilage. Soft-moist is packaged in daily amounts; however, the rest should be kept dry and free from rodents and insects. Dry dog food is best stored cool in a rodent proof, dry and sealed container. Metal, or plastic containers work well. The pails with lids that bakeries and restaurants discard after getting their ingredient supplies are ideal. Once we have opened the paper bag, we should empty the contents into one of these air tight, moisture resistant, and vermin proof containers.

GUIDELINES FOR FEEDING

"If a certain hound stays in good condition on one cup of meal and one tablespoonful of suet, than that's his proper ration. If he is running a good deal and losing condition, he should be fed more. SO, feed the hounds according to their needs, not according to a schedule on the package of food."
George D. Whitney, D.V.M. *This is the Beagle.*

What should we feed our dog?

As owners we must feed our dog enough of the required nutrients for the particular stage in life.

All the commercial dog foods on the market today, with few exceptions, can feed our dog to the maintenance level. It will provide the number of calories and other nutrients needed to maintain the body weight of a healthy adult dog at rest in a stress free and comfortable environment. This would include most of our average house pets. Once our dog moves from this type of situation, nutrient requirements change. A growing puppy, a pregnant mother, an active working dog or a sick convalescing individual will require much more. These individuals, we shall discuss later in Part Four. Some commercial dog food manufacturers have made products specifically for such individuals.

Kinds of Dog Food Available

- Maintenance: adult, constant weight, reasonably active
- Puppy: growth, active
- Reproduction and Lactation: mother and nursing
- Active: physical exertion, working
- Less Active: overweight, older, contained
- Special: illness, chronic disease condition

These dog foods are formulated to provide our dogs with foods that are more specific to their age or life style.

The average house pet is not too active, growing or working hard in a harsh environment. Most are free of much stress. This dog will do well on the maintenance level.

From the direction on the container, we can calculate the amount of dogfood that we should give per day. Use the maintenance level that the company suggests for our dog's weight. This is the best place to start; later on we may have to make changes. We said before and must repeat again, all dogs are individuals. The variation among dogs is greater than among people. Dogs come in all shapes and sizes and all temperaments. Foods are manufactured and recommended for an average dog. We must feed according to the dog responses and change if necessary.

How should we feed?

Have clean fresh water available at all times. An exception to this might be when house training puppies. Feed and water in a quiet place where the dog will not be disturbed.

The best bowls for water and food are easy to clean and resistant to wear and chewing. Soft plastic may be chewed and broken pieces swallowed. Pottery may chip and crack. Use non-toxic and non corrosive materials for the bowls and rinse well after washing with soap or other cleaners.

If the dog has a long nose and long ears use a narrow dish with high sides so that his or her ears will not get wet when drinking. Puppies and short nose dogs like a low flat dish.

Each dog, if more than one is in the household, should have its own food dish. While dogs can share a water bowl, if each has its own food dish, they will not be as prone to gulping their food. Some dogs may bloat or get a twisted stomach from gulping down food in a hurry. We must be especially careful with the barrel chested breeds like Labs and German Shepherds. Gastric torsions and other intestinal accidents can happen after eating too fast, with a lot of water, or right after vigorous exercise.

To prevent bloat, and some of these other problems, feed smaller portions and do not exercise or give a lot of water right after eating. Allow some time for rest after eating. Look for foods labeled "non expandable, and avoid the extruded (puffed up) products.

Use a measuring cup, glass or can to dish out dry food, so we can keep track of how much we feed. Warm refrigerated or cold food to body temperature if appetite is off.

Do not feed before car or air travel as these can be upsetting. Allow several hours before travel is planned.

If the dog is fussy, take food away; try later, but be watchful as the dog may be ill. If normally fussy, feed at regular times and avoid snacks. Train the dog; don't allow the dog to train you.

How Often Do We Feed?

We can leave food out continuously, free choice, or have a scheduled, restricted method of feeding. Each has its advantages and disadvantages, and each will depend upon our dog and our home situation.

Free choice: The dog's bowl is filled with food, more than can be consumed in a day, and is available at all times. The dog can eat whenever it wants. This is nice in that it takes less work and knowledge on our part. There is less aggression, often having a quieting effect when a group of dogs are fed. Some dogs may eat too much; however, with this method. We also tend to be less observant, and several days may go by with the dog not eating, before we realize that the dog is off his feed. If this was due to illness or diet problems, we may have lost valuable time. Dry dogfood or soft moist is more suited to this method, as opposed to canned or fresh recipes.

Should we decide to use the free choice method as it may suit our personal situation, if we are not home at regular times, there are a few guide lines to follow. When starting, feed the calculated amount on the package for one day. When this has been eaten, fill the bowl again. Always have food in the bowl and do not take it away after this. This initial procedure helps to prevent engorgement. Dogs will stop when their appetite is filled and realize they can slow down, and it is not necessary to gulp their food. Some dogs just may eat too much with food available at all times so will have to be limited. We may purchase dog foods higher in fiber content, that will fill the dog with more bulk, thereby reducing the number of calories eaten, and still keep him on free choice. Puppies, mothers, working and sick dogs are better fed on a scheduled program which we shall discuss later in their specific section. Free choice feeding can work well with adult dogs requiring the maintenance level of nutrients in a fairly constant environment.

Scheduled feeding: Here we restrict the amount of food or the time the food is left out. This takes more work. We have to be there to feed or have someone do it for us. We also have to be more knowledgeable because we are making the decision as to how much our dog will eat and when. Having this control, we can make observations with regard to health, appetite, condition and attitude and make changes when necessary.

For an adult dog on the maintenance level, twice a day feeding is believed to be the best for the dog. Feeding morning and evening gives the dog a shorter time between meals which will not load his digestive system all at once and also limit begging and whining between meals. The anticipation of regular feeding times also stimulates his appetite so that he cleans up his bowl.

Once a day feeding can work for some dogs depending on the individual and level of activity. This may suit our situation and does work well with some dogs.

We can also limit the time that we allow the food to be present. Ten minutes is enough time for a normal adult dog to clean up his daily portion.

Expectant and nursing mothers, toy breeds, growing puppies, working dogs or dogs out in cold temperatures should be fed at least three or more times a day. These individuals require more nutrients, especially energy, and do not have the stomach capacity to hold enough food at one time to last them very long. By feeding them more often, their greater requirements are met without overloading their systems. More on this later.

These are some guidelines on how often we should feed. Each dog is different and we all have different personal situations. Pick a method that will suit the dog for his requirements and our own time constraints. Train the dog. Let's not allow the dog to train us! This can happen if we give snacks between meals. Soon the dog learns that begging and whining pays off, as he has trained us to feed him when he asks. He now loses his appetite at meal time and we wonder why.

What we might want to try is to time the feeding times and toilet times soon after. Animals have what is called an "oral/anal reflex" which simply means that shortly after eating or drinking, they want to defecate or urinate. By taking advantage of this reflex, we can make house-training puppies easier.

Remember, a healthy dog can fast for a week or more without food but must have water. Fasting, or going without food for long periods of time, was a natural occurrence in the wild before man came along. If our dog should refuse to eat what we think is an appropriate diet with nothing else offered for two or three days, perhaps a visit to the veterinarian is in order in case something medically is wrong.

Don't whine or nag for the dog to eat. Put food down and leave the dog alone. After five to ten minutes take the bowl away.

The ideal amount of food to give our dog is that amount that will keep him in hard muscular condition with a thin layer of fat over his ribs.

The correct amount will be that amount that maintains:

- body weight at the desired level
- body condition: fat cover, muscle tone and hair coat
- activity level: energy to live and play

It is better, from the health standpoint of our dog, to underfeed rather than overfeed. Using calculations and rules of thumb on the amounts to feed can take away from the prime indicator which is our dog. How is he or she faring with this dog food and this amount? The dog tells us how much we should give it. Try not to fall into the idea that our dog's bowl should be filled with as much food as we would eat. Our dog could be a sixth of our size and a tenth as active. The amount in the bowl must reflect this size and activity level difference.

Start out by feeding the stated directions on the container for one day. Give one half of this in the morning and the other half in the evening. Then watch the dog, and after a week, make an assessment.

Our dog is receiving the right amount if

- it is on the hungry side, eats everything in about five minutes
- we can feel its ribs and hip bones with a light covering of fat
- its tummy is tucked up when we stand above and look down
- its ribs are wider than the abdominal area
- its skin is loose and the hair is glossy and thick
- its activity level is high and temperament is happy and cheerful

In order to have such a dog

- we have done our home work with regards to purchasing and offering nutritious food
- the amount given is just enough to maintain condition and activity level
- we include between meal snacks in the whole picture, (give that much less in the evening if giving snacks)
- we don't give in to fussy eaters

The amount we feed our dog depends upon

- His or her individual requirements
- The nutrient value of the dogfood.

Dogs eat to satisfy their need for energy.

A formula you may want to try is to feed 1/12 of the dog's desired body weight in volume of food. For example a twelve pound dog would require one pound of bulk per day, a twenty-four pound dog will receive two pounds and so on. Remember, formulas are fine, but our dog is the indicator of how much we feed.

The correct amount will equal the amount that is necessary to maintain

- desired body weight
- desired body condition
- desired activity level

All breeds and ages of dogs benefit from exercise, both physical and mental. This is not a nutritional topic but is such an important part of the health and well being of our dogs that some points must be mentioned.

Just a few words about mental or brain activities. Our dogs need mind stimulation just as we do; hide and seek games, retrieving, coarsing, with command response and praise keep them healthy.

Physical and mental activity have been part of the dog's survival since the beginning of time. As a hunter, he had to think and move faster and quicker than his prey if he was to eat. Domestication brought a total dependence upon us for his food, such that he doesn't have to use his head or his body very much. This lack of exercise slows down all his body systems and shortens his life. We have seen how modern means of transportation and work saving devices have affected our own bodies. Our dogs today are no different.

Exercise retains muscle tone, maintains strong bones and keeps the joints flexible. Physical activity maintains a strong cardiovascular system which, in turn, supplies all the other systems with oxygen and nutrients. Exercise builds stamina and endurance and also keeps an old dog younger. If the dog's body is in tone and all systems active, illness and disease can be prevented. Time for convalescing is shortened. I don't believe that there is any argument against the benefits of some sort of physical activity for the maintenance of health and well being.

A few precautions are in order. Start out slowly, build up endurance, and don't over do it. Assume our dog is in good health and, if in doubt, ask our veterinarian. Be careful on hot and sunny days and avoid hot pavement or cement surfaces.

Hard surfaces for running on should be avoided. Early morning or later in the evening are good times for exercise during hot weather. If our dog should lag behind, breathing heavily, coughing or stumbling, stop. Cool off and wet his body, if necessary. In winter, watch for ice build up and road salt on the dog's feet. After, soaking and drying of the feet should be considered.

Any type of activity will be beneficial. Walking, running, swimming, retrieving and play all are good. The exercise should be done on a regular basis and geared to the type, condition and age of the dog. Be careful exercising puppies of the giant breeds, as overdoing it can affect their soft, growing bones. Dogs that are overweight and in poor condition should be started slowly in combination with a diet program. Those breeds that are prone to patella luxations, "trick knees", or back problems should not be asked to walk on their hind legs or jump to beg for treats, as this unnatural position puts added strain on these parts. Hunting breeds like lots of room with freedom to move.

If we have to exercise on busy streets or city sidewalks, the dog may have to be on a leash unless it is well trained. We have to consider others; a "poop and scoop" philosophy is mandatory.

Exercising on an empty stomach is best. Do not worry about his immediate energy requirements during exercise, as these will be delivered from his glucose and glycogen store. His blood, muscle and liver are all ready to supply the energy, and any undigested food in his stomach will just cause him trouble. As we discussed before, the large chested breeds might twist their stomach (gastric torsion) if exercised on a partially or full stomach. Allow some time before feeding after vigorous activity for these same reasons. Basic common sense and discretion should be used when we ask our dogs to do physical activities; however, some sort of exercise is beneficial, healthy and normal.

If we find that our dog is getting a lot of physical activity, refer to the section on working dogs where additional nutrient requirements and recipes are covered.

When we purchase commercial dog foods, it would be reasonable to conclude that we are buying based on cost and palatability. If the price was reasonable and our dog liked it, we bought it. Barring any obvious problem, such as loose stools or other major upset, we are happy. From a nutritional stand point, we now know that this is not enough. When we were children, candy tasted good, but we wouldn't have done very well if that was all we ate. Dogs must have a balanced diet containing all the required nutrients in forms that are acceptable.

All dog foods are not the same. Just like many other things that we buy, there is a big difference between brands. We also must not fall into the trap (that advertising promotes) that more is better. We may be lead to believe that more protein, or more fiber, for example, is best. Our dog tells us what is best. We must observe the signs.

Manufactured dog food is a mixture of food and other ingredients combined to provide the dog with all his needs. By using the NRC recommendations for the amounts of each nutrient, manufacturers formulate a recipe of ingredients, add preservatives, antioxidants and flavors or flavor enhancers. Depending on ingredient sources and costs, including processing and packaging, the final product is made and priced accordingly. If the ingredients are all present in the minimum amounts, and the correct proportion, the product is sold as complete and balanced.

Often the manufacturers will put in more than the minimum amounts of nutrients to be on the safe side. Ingredients vary in their nutrient content. The volume of food a dog can eat in a day is important in the selection of the ingredients. All of the required nutrients must be present for the daily portion to be complete and balanced.

We must be confident in the product. By reading the label, examining the food, we go ahead and feed according to the directions. Since every dog is an individual with varying needs, we continue to observe and make changes, if necessary, either to the amount or the brand, or by supplementing with other foods.

Possible Problems with Commercial Dog Foods

- convenience leads to over feeding and obesity
- lack of nutrients can lead to poor growth and health
- continual use of one brand can lead to deficiencies
- cost not quality of nutrient is a prime concern
- inadequate or incomplete knowledge of canine nutrition on the part of the manufacturer
- minimum may not be adequate for all dogs
- uniform standards are quite basic.
- are the amounts of vitamins or minerals listed?
- nutritional claims are not backed up with feeding trials
- manufacturers do not perform adequate feed trials
- processing and storage leads to losses of nutrients
- manufactured for the average dog when all are different
- long term effects of additives may not be fully known
- do they have a "use before" date like people food?
- are ingredients "Government Inspected" before manufacture?
- actual ingredients are not listed, so we really do not know what we are buying.
- by-product labeling is all-encompassing, covering a large range of possible ingredients
- uniformity suffers between batches; ingredients may change
- there are no standards for moisture content
- fats must be processed or treated for storage and shipping
- ingredients may have been contaminated before or after processing.
- the amount suggested to feed is only a guideline.
- quality control is up to each individual manufacturer
- errors in feed formulations
- the prime purpose is to sell more dog food.

PART THREE Getting Started

Our own Thing

We can do " our own thing "
with a little knowledge
  a little extra planning
  a little preparation
we can present our pets with meals that are
  cheaper
  free of additives and preservatives
  as fresh
  as nutritious
  as tasty
and with as much variety
  as the foods we serve our family.

" the dogs eat of the crumbs which fall from their master's table "
  Matthew XV verse 27

Now we are getting ready to start cooking! The quote from the Bible reminds us that dogs have been fed from our tables for many years. We can continue to feed from our tables, using a little modern knowledge and science.

Part III will look more like the "cookbooks" that we are familiar with. Ingredients are listed that we use in recipes for our dogs. The ingredients are all familiar. The format, measuring and equipment are the same. Ingredients that we do not use are not listed. Before we go any further, we must outline the basic canine differences as they apply to the type of ingredients and recipes we use.

BASIC CANINE DIFFERENCES

In preparing recipes for our dog, we have to consider the basic differences between them and us. For us, colour and appearance of food are important. Colour and appearance are not important to our dog; smell and texture are. We enjoy the aromas of food cooking but nothing like a dog does with his very sensitive nose.

The sense of smell is very acute in the dog. Scientists have concluded the dog has such a keen sense of smell because he has a larger area in his nose with more olfactory cells for this purpose. These are the specialized cells that smell. For the dog as hunter and scavenger, this asset is very valuable to his survival. This acute sense was not only used to smell and identify food, but also to recognize friends or enemies. Smell is also important in mating and identifying young. Experiments have shown that dogs can easily recognize some organic compounds even after being diluted down to one in one million. (1 ppm, 1 part/million)

Scientists also tell us that the sense of smell is used by the dog to identify foods it eats based on experiences from the past. These experiences, rather than taste, are important in that the number of taste buds present in the dog's mouth is quite low.

To repeat, taste is believed to be of less importance because there are such a small number of taste buds in the dog's mouth compared to the number of olfactory cells. Let's look at the total number of taste buds in several species: man 9,000 cells, dog 1,700, pig and goat 15,000, kitten 475, chicken 24 (taken from *Dukes' Physiology of Domestic Animals*).

We are able to differentiate sweet, sour, bitter, and salty. However, the dog has three responses: pleasant, unpleasant and indifferent. Each species of animal has a taste for those foods that are suitable for it. The dog, being a carnivore, would have tastes developed for its particular diet. Taste also varies a lot between individuals.

If the dog, as a carnivore, can smell very well, not taste too well, and sweet, sour, and salty are not important, we should feed accordingly. His carnivore diet for millions of years was flesh, fat, bones, stomach and intestinal contents combined with hair and feathers. Fat is tasty for the dog, as it is for us, because many flavours are fat soluble or fat type molecules. Sugar is not important to the dog, but some dogs, as we know, can develop a taste if trained. Salt is of less importance to the diet of the dog in that he does not perspire or sweat like we do to remove heat. When we perspire to keep cool, we lose salt. Dogs do perspire some through the pads of their feet. Since the dog can conserve salt better than we can, especially when the weather is warm, salt is not an important ingredient. In the wild, the dog acquired his salt requirements from his flesh diet. So many of our foods today have sodium in them that the addition of salt to a dog diet is unnecessary.

Spices and pepper, for example, are of no use in a dog's dish and, if anything, may be harmful to the lining of his stomach and intestine. Spicy left-overs should be avoided in a dog's menu.

The bones, hair and feathers that the wild dog consumes provide him with calcium and phosphorus minerals and the hair and feathers were the bulk or roughage. The minerals we have to replace with bonemeal, for example, and the roughage we can make up with fiber foods.

Therefore, what is important and what is unimportant to a dog?

Important	Unimportant
smell	sight
experience	color
texture	spices
fat	sugar
consistency	pepper
minerals	bones
roughage	salt

EVALUATING TABLE SCRAPS

Table scraps? What do we think of when we hear the words table scraps? I believe the food that is left over from our dining table that our family has not eaten is what we are referring to. We also have the "table scraps" of the food industry that is not used for people food but is processed, packaged and ends up as pet food. Either the scraps from our table or the scraps (by-products) from the food processing industry are edible foods that are eaten by our pets.

We shall discuss the table scraps or left overs from our table. Some people believe that our table scraps are better than the by-product, table scraps, of industry. Feeding our home left-overs may require some precautions.

- Fat is very tasty but also very powerful with calories.
- Avoid spices and salty left overs.
- Cooked vegetables are fine, but raw vegetables should be mashed or aged.
- Avoid raw fish (fine bones and thiaminase)
- Avoid potato sprouts (a toxin; solanine)
- Over-cooking leads to vitamin losses.
- Cooked bones become brittle; raw bones are better.
- Chocolate is poisonous to a dog (three oz of baking chocolate can kill a twenty lb dog)
- Avoid spicy chili, pepperoni or luncheon meats

Can Do's with table scraps

- Cook extra so that we have left-overs.
- Left-overs can be stored for several days and used a little at a time for flavour enhancing.
- Utilize left-overs in our recipes.
- Keep trimmings from meat, bread, vegetables and fruit, which can be used later in a recipe.
- Remember, spinach and rhubarb (oxalic acid) binds calcium.
- Dogs like garlic; use powder, liquid, or cloves, not salt.
- Feeding left-overs, up to twenty-five percent, with a quality commercial dog food will not affect the balance of nutrients appreciably.

Have a Left-Overs Container

A left-overs container or a "doggie bag" is a good idea, in my opinion. I use a plastic container with a loose cover that I set out and leave on the kitchen cupboard, not in the fridge. Dogs prefer aged food that is warm. Watch them burying food out in the back yard and come back to it later. The container is easily washed, and I store those left-overs that I consider good. I do not save spicy or salty foods. Fat, meat trimmings, vegetable and fruit trimmings, vegetable drainings, cheese trimmings will go into this container. If it is meat, fat, oils, or dairy products, I will add some of this directly to the commercial dry dog food that I normally feed. The amount of dry food will be less in volume depending upon the quality and the amount of left-overs. If the left-overs are vegetable and fruit trimmings, I puree this in the blender and let sit in the warm container for a day or two. I then feed this later, in the same way I would the fat or meat trimmings, or use in a recipe.

Remember the dog's short digestive system and his difficulty digesting vegetables and fruits. Sweet foods, cookies and cakes do not go in the dog dish. Understand, evaluate the left-overs from our knowledge of nutrients and foods and feed accordingly. Learn to identify the nutrients in the scraps. If primarily

> fat - add protein and carbohydrates.
> protein - add fat and carbohydrates.
> carbohydrate - add fat and protein.

Table scraps have been blamed for causing obesity in our pets. Perhaps this is true in some cases, but I believe pet obesity today is due to lack of exercise and over-feeding of our commercial dog foods. Our modern dogs do not get the exercise that our pets did several years ago. This is especially a concern with urban dogs. Commercial dog foods of good quality are so readily available and convenient that we over-feed. Years ago, the dog got the left-overs and maybe a homemade recipe if there was not enough left from the table. I think we see more obese dogs today because of the big boom and availability of commercial dog food coupled with a lack of exercise.

EQUIPMENT

Basic kitchen equipment will not vary from what we have in the kitchen now. If we are going to do a lot of cooking for our pets or if we have many to feed, we may want to have larger pots and storage facilities.

A list of commonly used kitchen equipment:

- sauce pan
- frying pan
- large soup kettle
- cake pans
- loaf or bread pans
- muffin tins
- ice cube trays
- pie pans
- cookie sheets
- casserole dish
- mixing bowls
- measuring cup
- measuring spoons
- metal spoon
- wooden spoon
- paring knife
- meat, bone saw
- food grinder, blender
- biscuit cutter
- rolling pin
- cutting board
- bucket
- refrigerator containers

The ingredients are listed with a view to their importance in a dog's diet and our awareness of their nutrient content. The predominate nutrients are listed with the greatest first. Letters A, B, B_{12}, C, D, E, refer to the vitamins.

Alfalfa sprouts	protein, fiber, C and minerals
Bacon	fat, protein, sodium
Beef	protein, fat, B_{12}, niacin, thiamin, riboflavin, iron
Bologna	fat, protein, sodium, B_{12}, minerals
Bones	minerals, calcium and phosphorus (ham bones, steak bones, knuckles, hocks)
Bonedust from butcher	bone, meat, fat, marrow, blood minerals, fat and protein
Bone meal ground bones	calcium, phosphorus, fluorine and other trace minerals
Bouillon cubes	sodium, carbohydrate
Brain	protein, fat, phosphorus, iron
Bran	(outer coat of the seed of cereal grains like wheat, rye, corn or rice, high in thiamine, and fiber)
Breads	carbohydrate, (often fortified with vitamins & minerals, not necessary to toast, starches are cooked already)
Bread crumbs	carbohydrate, fiber, sodium, B, iron
Brewers yeast	vitamin B complex, protein (12 amino acids) minerals, carbohydrate and fat
Brisket	fat, protein, B_{12}, B, zinc, iron
Bulgar	carbohydrate, protein, B, minerals
Butter	fat, A, D, E, sodium
Buckwheat pancakes	protein, E, sodium, minerals
Buttermilk	protein, riboflavin, B_{12}, calcium, sodium

Cereals	Brand name breakfast cereals:
All Bran ®	fiber, A, B, C, D, iron, minerals
Corn Flakes ®	carbohydrate, A, B, C, D, iron, sodium
Mueslix ®	fiber, carbohydrate, A, E, B, B_{12}, iron
Granola	carbohydrate, protein, fat, E, B, minerals
Oatmeal (cooked)	carbohydrate, protein, fat, fiber, B
Rice Krispes ®	carbohydrate, A, B, C, D, iron

Cheese	protein, fat, calcium, B_{12}, zinc
Chicken	protein, fat, E, B, B_{12}, minerals
Chicken liver	A, B_{12}, protein, C, B, E, iron, fat, zinc
Chili & Beans	protein, fat, B_{12}, C, B, E, A, iron,
Corn	(see vegetables)
Cornmeal	fiber, carbohydrate, B, sodium, iron
Corn oil	fat, E
Corn syrup	carbohydrate, iron
Cottage cheese	protein, fat, iron, B_{12}, B, calcium
Crackers	carbohydrate, fat
Cream	fat, carbohydrate,
Dandelion greens	carbohydrate, protein, sodium
Duck	protein, fat, E, B_{12}, B, iron, zinc
Eggs	protein, fat, D, E, B, B_{12}, iron
	(avidin in raw whites binds biotin)
Eggnog	fat, protein, A, D, riboflavin, B_{12}, calcium
Epsom salts	magnesium sulfate (magnesium source)
Fish	(see seafood)
	(cook to destroy thiaminase and worms)
Fish liver oil (cod liver oil)	only concentrated natural food sources of vitamin D and true vitamin A; also small amounts of phosphorus, iodine & sulfur

Flour	carbohydrate, protein, vitamins, minerals
Wholewheat	carbohydrate, protein, fiber, B, iron
Soy flour	protein, fat, fiber, thiamine, riboflavin, high in iron, calcium, potassium
Corn flour	carbohydrate, fiber, thiamine, iron
Buckwheat flour	carbohydrate, protein, fiber, thiamine, B_6 high in iron, potassium
All purpose	carbohydrate, protein, fiber, B, iron
Frankfurters	fat, protein, sodium
French toast	protein, fat, sodium, B_{12}, B, iron, minerals
Fruit (raw, cooked, stewed, dried)	
Apples	fiber, C, E, B, potassium
Apricots (dried)	A, E, potassium
Bananas	fiber, C, E, B_6, potassium
Berries	fiber, carbohydrate, C, E, B, potassium
Dates (dried)	fiber, carbohydrate, B, potassium, iron
Grapefruit	carbohydrate, C, E, B, potassium
Oranges	carbohydrate, C, E, B, potassium, calcium
Pears	carbohydrate, fiber, C, E, potassium
Prunes (dried)	fiber, carbohydrate, A, B, potassium, iron
Raisins	carbohydrate, fiber, E, B, potassium, iron
Garlic	carbohydrate, potassium, calcium (appetizer, digestive stimulant, powder, oil, cloves, not salt)
Grains (see flour)	energy, carbohydrate, protein, vitamins not more than 50% of Dry Matter of dog diet always, processed, cooked to break down starches
Granola	(see cereals)

Ham smoked	protein, fat, C, D, B, B_{12}, sodium, minerals
Hamburger	protein, fat, carbohydrate, B_{12}, B, E, iron
Honey	carbohydrate, riboflavin, iron, potassium
Hot Dog	fat, sodium, protein, C, B_{12}, B, minerals
Kidney	protein, B_{12}, B, A, iron, zinc, fat
Lamb	protein, fat, B_{12}, B, E, minerals
Lard pork	fat, E
Lentils	protein, C, E, B, iron, potassium
Lettuce	fiber, A, C, E, folate, potassium
Liver beef	protein, fat, A, B_{12}, B, C, D, E, iron, zinc *"miracle food"*, *"unidentified liver fractions"*, *"natures mystery food "*.....Dr. Collins

"If there is one single food that every dog should have in its diet, that food would have to be liver. It contains more nutrients in one package than any other natural food available to man or beast".....Dr. Collins, Dog Nutrition.

Macaroni	carbohydrate, protein, E, B, iron
Margarine	fat, A, D, E, sodium
Meat	protein, fat, vitamins and minerals,

Meat, or animal flesh, is easily and almost completely digested, all of the protein, and ninety-five percent of the fat. Raw meat requires about two hours for digestion whereas cooked to well-done may take four hours. Grade or colour does not affect the nutrient value.

Milk	carbohydrate, protein, fat, vitamins & minerals
(skim, whole, condensed)	(Adults may have hard time digesting lactose. Most store purchased is fortified with vitamins)
Muffin Bran	fat, carbohydrate, fiber, sodium, B, iron
Nuts	fat, protein, vitamin E and some B's
Millet	carbohydrate, protein, fiber, thiamine, minerals

Oats	carbohydrate, protein, B, magnesium, iron
Oils	fat, essential fatty acids, E
Onion	C, minerals
Onion powder	carbohydrate, potassium, calcium, magnesium
Peanut Butter	fat, protein, E, niacin,
Parsley	C, folate, iron, potassium, calcium
Pasta	carbohydrate, protein, E, B, iron
Popcorn	carbohydrate
Pork	protein, fat, B, B_{12}, iron, zinc
Potatoes	(see vegetables)
Potato Pancakes	fat, carbohydrate, B, E, sodium
Rabbit	protein, B_{12}, B, iron, minerals
Rice brown	carbohydrate, fiber, E, minerals
Salt	sodium (Sea Salt, sodium chloride plus iodine)
Sausage	fat, protein, sodium, B_{12}, B, minerals
Sea Food	
Fish Sticks	protein, fat, E, B, B_{12}, potassium
Cod fried	protein, fat, E, B, B_{12}, potassium, sodium
Oysters Eastern	high B_{12} & zinc, iron, A, D, C, E, B
Salmon canned	protein, fat, high D & B, E, calcium, iron
Shrimp canned	protein, cholesterol, D, E, B, B_{12}
Tuna canned oil	protein, fat, iron, sodium
Seeds Sunflower	fat, high E, B
Soups	dehydrated high in sodium
Beef/Barley	protein, fat, carbohydrate, A, B_{12}, sodium
Chicken Noodle	protein, A, B, sodium, iron
Chicken Rice	protein, fat, A, B, sodium, iron
Consomme	protein, potassium, sodium, iron
Minestrone	protein, carbohydrate, fat, A, B, sodium
Onion	B, sodium, potassium
Steak round	protein, fat, B_{12}, B, iron, zinc, potassium
Swiss cheese	protein, fat, calcium, B_{12}, D, zinc
Tofu	protein, fat, E, B, magnesium, iron, calcium
Tomato Paste	carbohydrate, A, C, B, sodium, potassium, iron
Tongue	protein, fat, B_{12}, B, iron, zinc

Tripe	protein, fat (the muscular lining of the four stomachs of cattle and sheep)
Turkey	protein, fat, B_{12}, B, E, zinc, iron, potassium
Turkey roll	protein, fat, sodium, B, minerals
Veal	protein, fat, B_{12}, zinc, iron, potassium
Vegetables	(cooked)
Asparagus	protein, carbohydrate, C, E, B, minerals
Baked Beans	protein, carbohydrate, fiber, A, B, minerals
Green Beans	fiber, carbohydrate, C, B, potassium, iron
Lima Beans	fiber, protein, high E, B, minerals
Beets	fiber, E, C, B, potassium, iron
Broccoli	fiber, protein, C, A, E, B, calcium, magnesium
Brussel sprouts	fiber, carbohydrate, protein, C, E, B, iron
Cabbage	fiber, C, E, B, minerals
Carrots	carbohydrate, C, E, B, minerals
Cauliflower	fiber, C, B, minerals
Celery	fiber, C, B, potassium
Corn	carbohydrate. fiber, protein, C, E, B
Cucumber (raw)	C, E, B, potassium
Mushrooms (raw)	fiber, C, E, B, potassium, iron
Parsnips	fiber, carbohydrate, C, E, B, minerals
Peas	fiber, carbohydrate, protein, C, B, potassium
Spinach	fiber, carbohydrate, protein, A, C, E, B, iron
Turnips	fiber, carbohydrate, A, C, E, B, potassium
Zucchini	fiber, A, C, B, potassium
Vegetable oil	fat, E
Venison	protein, vitamins and minerals
Waffles	fat, carbohydrate, D, E, B_{12}, B, sodium
Wheat germ oil	fat, all vitamin E s, B, A and fatty acids (extract of the wheat germ)
Yogurt	protein, fat, B_{12}, riboflavin, calcium
Yeast dry	protein, B especially thiamine & riboflavin, calcium, iron

DOROSZ 93

Bath Time!

Ingredients that can be picked up at a Health Food Store

alfalfa tablets	protein, beta-carotene, calcium
alfalfa powder	protein, vitamins, minerals
bone meal	calcium and phosphorus
blackberry leaves	for pregnant bitches
bran	fiber, thiamine
Brewers yeast	B vitamins
Cod-liver oil	vitamins A and D
dessicated liver powder	vitamins, protein
dicalcium phosphate	calcium and phosphorus
dried fish	protein, fat soluble vitamins
dried sea weed	minerals, vitamins
dried spinach	iron, vitamins, protein
glandular organ powder	protein, vitamins
Infant liquid vitamins	vitamins for small dogs
kelp powder	minerals (iodine)
"Lite salt"	regular salt & potassium chloride
raspberry leaves	for pregnant bitches
vitamin B complex	B vitamins
vitamin C	powder or tablets ascorbic acid or sodium ascorbate
vitamin D	capsules
vitamin E	capsules
wheat germ	vitamin E
yeast	B vitamins

add our own

....
....
....
....
....
....
....
....
....

NUTRIENT COMPARISONS OF INGREDIENTS

The classes of ingredients are listed for some of the basic nutrients. The food on the top of the list contains the highest amount, then the next highest and so on down the list.

PROTEIN

Beef & Game	Pork, Veal & Lamb	Poultry
venison	leg of lamb	turkey diced
rabbit	calf liver	chicken diced
round roast lean	ham	chicken breast
steak lean	lamb chops	goose
chili with beans	veal cutlets	chicken liver
kidney	pork butt	pheasant
tongue	ham canned	duck

Dairy & Eggs	Cooked Grains	Cooked Vegetables
quiche	oat bran	beans (all)
omelette	millet	tofu
cottage cheese	rice bran	peas
yogurt	bulgur	lentils
goat milk	rice	spinach
cow milk	corn	potatoes

FAT

Meat	Dairy and Eggs	Butter and Oils
brisket	quiche	corn oil
corn beef	omelette	olive oil
meat loaf	goat milk	vegetable oil
ground lamb	cheddar cheese	pork lard
duck	whole milk	margarine
tongue	egg	butter

CARBOHYDRATE

Cooked Grains
millet
oat bran
rice
bulgur
corn grits

Cooked Vegetables
sweet potatoes
beans
corn
potatoes
carrots

Cereals
Raisin Bran ®
Rice Krispies ®
Cream of Wheat ®
oatmeal
Corn Flakes ®

FIBER

Cooked vegetables
beans (all)
peas
parsnips
corn
broccoli

Fruit
berries
dried prunes
raisins
apples
oranges

Cereals
All Bran ®
Mueslix ®
Bran Flakes ®
oat bran, cooked
oatmeal, cooked

VITAMINS

Vitamin A
cod liver oil
liver
carrots
sweet potato
spinach
margarine

Vitamin D
cod liver oil
salmon
sardines in oil
milk (fortified)
chicken liver
Swiss cheese

Vitamin E
wheat germ oil
sunflower seeds
vegetable oil
corn oil
sweet potato
beans, all

MINERALS

Calcium
bonemeal
yogurt
milk
sardines
salmon
Fava beans

Zinc
Oysters Eastern
beef shank
liver
beef ground
lamb
pork

Sodium
salt
smoked ham
soups dried
bouillon cube
luncheon meats
wieners

UNDERSTANDING THE MEASUREMENTS

Measurements for the dog recipes are the same as those in any cookbook. You will note in some recipes that when the measurements are converted to metric, ounces may be converted to mL when it really should be to gm. As cooks, this eliminates the need for us to weigh an ingredient and use a volume measurement like a tsp. or tbsp. Strictly speaking mL are used for volume measurements of liquids; powders and solids are measured and weighed in grams. For example 8 oz. may be converted as 250 mL.

From my experiences with animal health students and animal owners there sometimes is confusion with regards to the various metric measurements; therefore, I have included this outline.

METRIC (milli = 1/1000th., centi = 1/100th. & kilo = 1000)

WEIGHT	milligrams		grams		kilograms
	1 mg.	=	.001 gm.	=	.000001 kg.
	1000 mg.	=	1 gm.	=	.001 kg.
	1000000 mg.	=	1000 gm.	=	1 kg.

LIQUID	milliliters		liters
	1000 mL	=	1 L
	1 mL	=	.001 L

LENGTH					
millimeters	centimeters		meters		kilometers
1000mm. =	100 cm.	=	1 m.	=	.001 km.
100mm. =	1 cm.	=	.01 m.	=	.00001 km.
1mm. =	.01 cm.	=	.0001 m.	=	.000001 km.

VOLUME a cubic centimeter (cc) = a cube: 1 cm/ 1 cm/ 1 cm
The standard used is water;

weight		liquid		volume
1 gram	=	1 milliliter	=	1 cubic centimeter of water
(1 gm	=	1 mL	=	1 cc. of water)

All ingredients other than water will either weigh more or less for the same volume. Non liquids like powders and solids will also vary. For example, oils are lighter than water; that is why they float to the top. 1 mL of oil = 1 cc. but will weigh less than 1 gm. Mercury, a very heavy liquid, the volume of 1 mL = 1 cc but weighs much more than 1 gm.

"Good cooking means the knowledge of all fruits, herbs, balms and spices, and all that is healing and sweet in fields and groves, and savory in meats. It means carefulness, inventiveness, watchfulness, willingness and readiness of appliances. It means the economy of your great-grandmothers and the science of modern chemists."
    Ruskin

"Cooking is a science that involves physics and chemistry, but it is also an Art that involves all five of our senses."
    Barbara Hill

A dog eats food that smells right and will fill his or her basic requirement for energy. Appetite governs the basic urge to fulfill these needs. This primitive instinct (hunger) to ingest food is the way dogs will obtain the nutrients they require. With our knowledge of nutrition, we give dogs the nutrients in various combinations or recipes so that they can live long and healthy lives. As stated earlier, this is solely our responsibility as our dogs cannot go out and "hunt" for those nutrients that may be lacking.

Recipes in this section were developed and tested using nutritionally sound ingredients. Many of the recipes are modifications of recipes for us. There is no reason that you cannot make up recipes yourselves if you take into consideration the basic differences between us and the nutrient contents of the ingredients. If you should have a favorite recipe and would like to share it with us, there is a section at the end of the book that tells you how to do this.

Recipes are for our modern dog on a maintenance requirement, that is to say, a dog that is fully grown, in good body condition, with moderate exercise and under no stress. They are not intended for a growing puppy, a nursing mother, or a working, sporting dog. Individuals such as these have different special needs.

Before we get to the Special Recipes for those dogs with added nutritional requirements, we will outline four areas that I have called Traditional, Natural, Price Conscious, and Gourmet. Again these are for the "average" pet on a maintenance level.

Traditional refers to how we may be feeding our dog today. We buy what we believe to be a good commercial dog food, and we might add left-overs or throw something else in. We might even have a recipe or two that we use. We may have doubts about this method, but up until now, our dog does not seem to be suffering and enjoys the change. In this section, I have followed this same "traditional" approach with guidelines where necessary.

Natural, Health Conscious or Holistic recipes are for those of us who would like to feed our dog ourselves. We want to use foods that are either fresh or not processed, trying to get away from the commercially prepared dog foods. Here we discuss this approach and offer recipes that we might try.

The price conscious, economy and bulk section is presented for the dog feeder who may want to economize for whatever reason. We may have more than one dog and would still like to supply all the required nutrients but ease up on the grocery budget.

Gourmet is where we have some fun. Indulge in some fancy recipes for those special occasions: birthdays, Thanksgiving, Christmas or just let our hair down and enjoy. Why shouldn't our dogs have these same opportunities as well? With these recipes we are not as concerned with cost, calories or nutrients but good taste. These recipes are not meant to become a routine but rather a time for enjoyment and a culinary gift to our best friend.

To repeat, the type of dog we are feeding is the dog on a maintenance level of nutrition, the typical house pet that most of us have, a dog that is reasonably active, in fair body condition and leading a normal stress free life, "our pet".

Let's Play

What does the traditional Dog owner feed? Probably a commercial dog food with or without table scraps (left-over people food).

Tradition today involves purchasing either a bag or a number of cans from the supermarket, taking this home and giving it to our pet in an amount that we think they will clean up. We may or may not give left-overs, or bones from the family table. We may feed once, twice a day, or we may just fill up the dog dish and refill it when it's empty. Our dog may have a preference for one brand in particular; maybe this is too expensive, so we have convinced him that a dry food in a bag is also tasty, good for him and cheaper for us. Perhaps our dog is a little overweight and our veterinarian has suggested our dog should lose some weight. Since he has been neutered and will not be as active, he will not need as much. We say "Gee we don't feed much now, just what's left over from the kids and us, mixed with some dried dog food that we picked up at the supermarket". The good doctor then suggests that our pet go on a reducing diet and may suggest a special diet that we should feed and nothing else. This is fine, but it seems that we are spending more money now on dog food than we did before and really have not noticed any weight loss.

We may have just purchased a puppy or someone has given us one and now we have to feed it. The pup is still growing and we want to do everything right. Or we have a female and have had her bred, and we are concerned that she have the adequate nutrients during her pregnancy and nursing stage. What do we do?

These may be events that we have had to deal with. We may have dealt with them in the traditional manner, but maybe we didn't understand what we were doing completely or still have some concerns. For these special individuals refer to the Special Recipes section starting on page 177.

There are excellent commercially prepared pet foods on the market today. There are also poor ones. Some companies spend many dollars on nutritional research, manufacturing techniques and on flavour and storage chemistry, so that we the consumers have some quality products to buy. Refer to Part II for more details on commercial dog foods. Especially read the summary and problems we may encounter with commercial dog foods on page 115.

The following recipes will utilize commercial dog food and table scraps. Again refer to Evaluating Table Scraps on page 120 for precautions. Rather than discarding left-overs, we can use them for the nutrients and flavours they have. We may not have the time to prepare the complete meal so we use a good quality dog food that we have bought. Some of us just may not like to cook.

The object is to "stretch out" the commercial dog food while adding some fresh home ingredients. We might use commercially prepared people foods such as cereals and soups in these recipes. We always pay attention to the amount that we give, by mentally calculating the kind and amounts of left-overs we are giving and then reducing the amount of commercial dog food accordingly. If the table scraps contain a lot of fat, remember fat has over two times the amount of calories of other foods, so cut back on the other. In other words we are always watching the amount of calories we give. Most dog nutritionists and dog feeders agree that we can replace twenty-five percent of a good quality commercial dog food with other foods and not disturb the balance appreciably.

You will note that many of the recipes call for B complex and vitamin C. These vitamins are water soluble and are very easily lost when foods are heated and stored for any length of time. By reading the labels of commercial dog foods, we see that these vitamins may not be replaced after processing. Since B's and C are water soluble, the dangers due to over dosing are not a concern in that the extra is eliminated by the dog.

BACON 'N' EGG PORRIDGE BREAKFAST

Pan fry this breakfast that will last all day.

Bacon, slices	**3**	**3**
Eggs	**2**	**2**
Oatmeal	**1 cup**	**250 mL**
Milk	**1/4 cup**	**50 mL**

Chop the bacon into 1/2 inch pieces and fry in a pan. Add the oatmeal until brown. Remove from the pan and add the milk and well beaten eggs. When the eggs are just about done, pour back the bacon and oatmeal stirring the while to finish. Cool and put into the dog's dish. Serves a 50 lb (23 kg) dog a hearty breakfast.

This is an excellent way to start the day, with protein, energy and vitamins.

LEFTOVER OMELET

A good way to use leftover beef, chicken, turkey or pork.

Leftover meat	**4-6 oz**	**125-170 gm**
Eggs	**2**	**2**
Vegetable oil	**2 tbsp**	**30 mL**

Chop the meat scraps and fry in the oil. Beat the eggs gently and pour over the meat and continue frying. Cool and cut into pieces, feed as is, or mix with equal portions of dry dog food, rice or mashed potatoes or other carbohydrate ingredient.

The vitamin mineral supplements on page 150 and 151 can be used to provide additional vitamins and minerals.

Restaurant, Doggie Bag, Left-overs

We often have the opportunity to take home "Doggie Bag" left-overs home with us after eating out. This has become socially acceptable as frugality is "in". Most restaurants will "bag" the left-overs when asked.

Typical foods we can consider to take home for Fido:

- larger blunt bones, steak, chops, ribs
- trimmed fat and skin
- meat, left-over hamburgers and hot dogs, (leave chili)
- potatoes, rice, pasta and French fries
- vegetables, (leave those with spicy or salty sauces)
- breads, buns, (leave sweet desserts, cakes and pies)
- take home cheese cakes, (leave ice creams and chocolate)
- take home pizza

When we get home, refrigerate the doggie bag and plan the next days menu around the left-overs. Identify what we have brought home with regards to the main nutrient present. Fat and skin is fat with spices; rice, pasta, vegetables and breads are carbohydrate; meats and cheese are protein and fat. French fries are carbohydrate and fat.

Use the various left-overs either with other ingredients or the regular dog food. Remember to reduce the amount of dog food accordingly when adding fats and carbohydrates. Bones are fine.

The size and type of dog will determine the size and kind of bones that we give. Small rib bones from sweet and sour ribs for example can be chewed up by most dogs. The smaller the dog the bigger the bone. They are less likely to chew or swallow a big bone whole. If the dog takes the time to chew cooked bones like rib bones they do quite well and are very good.

A pasta treat that is wholesome and nutritious.

Macaroni or pasta, cooked	**4 1/2 cups**	**1 L**
Beef, pork, chicken or lamb		
** roast drippings**	**1 cup**	**500 mL**
Garlic powder	**1/4 tsp.**	**1 mL**
Liver pate	**2 tbsp.**	**30 mL**

Put the cooked macaroni or pasta into a casserole dish. Pour the drippings on top and sprinkle with the garlic powder. Bake at 350⁰ F
(180⁰ C) for about 20 - 30 minutes. Cool and spread pate over the top.

Slice and serve cold with regular dog food as a treat.

Fido's very own pizza.

Frozen pizza dough	**1**	**1**
Tomato paste	**1/3 cup**	**75 mL**
Water	**1/3 cup**	**75 mL**
Vegetable oil	**1 tbsp.**	**15 mL**
Kelp	**1 tsp.**	**5 mL**

Toppings: pieces of left-over meats, fish (watch for bones) cheeses, garlic cloves, cooked vegetables, salad trimmings.

Mix up the 4 ingredients and spread over the defrosted pizza dough. Cut up the toppings into small pieces and spread. Bake at 400⁰ F (200⁰ C) for 20-25 minutes.

Cool, slice and serve according to size of dog.

Sauces

These "sauces" can be made before hand and poured onto commercial dog food or vegetable or cereal type table scraps.

GRAVY

Gravy, left-over	2 cups	500 mL
Bone dust or Bone meal (minerals)	1 tbsp.	15 mL
Vitamin C powder (or 500 mg crushed tablet)	1 tbsp.	15 mL
Brewers yeast (B complex)	1 tbsp.	15 mL
Wheat germ oil (vitamin E)	1 tbsp.	15 mL

Mix into a 2 1/2 cup container. Add as topping to dry dog food or left overs for flavour, vitamins and minerals. Amount will vary with the size of the dog.

SOUR CREAM GARLIC SAUCE

Sour cream	2 cups	500 mL
Garlic powder	2 tbsp.	30 mL
Vitamin C powder (or 500 mg crushed tablet)	1 tbsp.	15 mL
Brewers yeast (B complex)	1 tbsp.	15 mL
Wheat germ oil (vitamin E)	1 tbsp.	15 mL

Mix and use as toppings for dry dog food, table scraps, or home made dog biscuits.

The "red wine" recipe on page 173 can be used over dry dog food and other recipes for their flavour enhancement and for their nutritious contents.

Traditional recipes use commercial dog foods and left-overs to advantage. By using our imagination to provide variety, we can do many things to the regular dog food.

DOROSZ 93

NATURAL, HEALTH CONSCIOUS, HOLISTIC RECIPES

As Consumers we are Looking For

fresh and wholesome,
natural or homemade,
free of additives and preservatives,
convenient and quick,
good value, quality and taste,
and environmentally friendly food products.

It has been said the "Dog is man's best friend." Do we treat him or her as our best friend? If we should have friends of our own species over to visit, we offer food and drink as part of our friendship. We go to great lengths; witness the large number of human recipes books offering tasty colourful dishes to please our guests and we eagerly await any compliments. We become very disturbed if a special recipe does not turn out or we feel that it just wasn't right.

Now we have our best friends living with us and how do we treat them? The same old dish day in and day out. Or do we offer some variety which includes freshness and flavour? Do we tease our friends, who have an excellent sense of smell, with aromas from the backyard barbecue and kitchen, and then say "No", go and eat your dried biscuit, but I'll still be your friend?

I believe with some basic knowledge of canine nutrition and a little imagination, we can offer healthy and enjoyable meals for our four-legged friends. We can then watch the compliments as our friends display their enjoyment right to the tip of their wagging tails.

The general consensus is that the Asiatic wolf (Canis lupus pallipes) is the ancestor of our domestic dog. Our domestic dog (Canis familaris) is believed to have been domesticated about 10,000 to 12,000 years ago.

Being a hunter, survival for the ancestral dog was based on what he could catch or find. This not only required physical exertion but also offered a choice. As we have said earlier, the dogs of these early days ate the complete prey. Observing the wild cousins of our domestic dog today, we note that they go for the internal organs: liver, pancreas and kidney first. We also observe that they consume the stomach and intestinal contents as well as the muscle and bones. It is interesting that they eat the meat or "steak" later and tend to eat the organs first.

Our dog and the wild canines have adapted to their environment over millions of years. On the other hand, the dog is also able to change and adapt to different environments and diets; however, these changes cannot be great and adapting takes a long of time. Dogs can survive as an omnivore, as opposed to a strict carnivore such as the cat. Omnivores receive nutrition from animal and plant sources, and we know that the wild dogs do consume semi-processed plant material when they eat of the stomach and intestinal contents of their prey. If we are to feed our dog in a natural, organic, and holistic manner, we take all these considerations into our plans.

Just a few words about a canine vegetarian diet. This type of diet is possible; however, I believe there is no known benefit or advantage. I base this on the type of diet he ate for many years and his particular adapted digestive system for this diet. Refer to page 23 and the section on Our Pet's Basic Digestion and Absorption. Vegetables, fruits, and cereals alone are hard for him to utilize. Balancing the diet for all necessary nutrients becomes quite difficult considering his shorter digestive system and lack of room for prolonged bacterial digestion. Herbivores, plant eaters, are built differently so that they can, in fact, eat large amounts of these foods. Lastly, dogs aren't particularly fond of these foods and getting them to eat strictly plant food in large enough quantities to get all of their requirements becomes a challenge and a great burden on their nature. A total vegetarian diet is unnatural and stressful on their system.

Many of us, including pet owners, are becoming more and more concerned with the foods we, our families and our pets eat. This leads to questions about preservatives, pesticides, herbicides, additives and residues in our foods. Prepared foods that have been processed and altered to prevent spoilage and maintain shelf live fill our shelves. We buy fresh items that we can eat soon to compliment the commercially prepared foods. If we want to do the same for our pets, it will require some effort and some basic knowledge, but the task is not impossible.

Terms like "natural," "organic", and "additive free" will be defined in specific terms, so we all know what is meant by their use in advertising and labeling. For example: The Association of American Feed Control Officials (AAFCO) defines the term natural as *"of or pertaining to a product wholly comprised of ingredients completely devoid of artificial or man made substances, including, but not necessarily limited to, synthetic flavors, colors, preservatives, vitamins, minerals, or other additives, whether added directly to the product or incidentally as a component of another ingredient"*. We may have seen these terms used loosely on labels today; however, in the future, as labeling laws catch up, they will be defined and meaningful.

Cooking vs Raw

Just a few comments on this ongoing debate. Raw is obviously more "natural" as the dogs of old and in the wild didn't cook their food before they ate it. However, their food was cleaner in that it was killed relatively recent and not exposed to too many other things by the time it was eaten. Foods today have great opportunity for contamination from many sources before our dog will get to eat them, so cooking is important to kill bacteria that may cause disease. Some sort of processing is required for the vegetable and cereal ingredients, much like the digestion undergone in the stomach and intestines of the captured prey. Cooking makes digestion easier because some breakdown has been started; however, as we have said before, some nutrients are lost. We must replace these lost nutrients then after cooking.

Preparing a complete diet at home can be relatively easy when balancing for proteins, fats, carbohydrate and fiber. Vitamin and mineral formulating is a little more involved. To be sure that we have adequate vitamins and minerals we can use a prepared supplement or make one ourselves from ingredients that we assemble. As we have discussed in other parts of the book, understanding what nutrients are present in the foods that we offer our dog and which ones are not or are lost due to cooking, is a concern. For those nutrients, in particular vitamins that are lost, must be replaced.

Here are some recipes for vitamin mineral supplements that can be given to ensure that our dog is receiving the requirements.

Vitamin, Mineral Supplements

These recipes, one a dry supplement and the other a liquid supplement, can be prepared in advance and given every day. Do not give both at the same time. Use the dry or the liquid.

DRY SUPPLEMENT

Brewer's yeast (B vitamins)	2 cups	500 mL
Dessicated liver powder		
(A,D, & iron)	1 cup	250 mL
Bone meal or bone dust		
(Ca, & P)	1 cup	250 mL
Sunflower seeds, ground fine		
(E & B)	1 cup	250 mL
Sodium ascorbate (C)	1/2 cup	125 mL
Garlic powder (flavour)	2 tbsp.	30 mL

Mix all of these ingredients together and store in an air tight container in the refrigerator. Give 1/2 tsp. for toy dogs, 1 tsp for medium size dogs to 1 tbsp for large dogs. Cut the recipe in half for small dogs, so that the preparation stays fresher.

LIQUID SUPPLEMENT

Wheat germ oil (vitamin E)	1/4 cup	50 mL
Cod liver oil (vitamins A and D)	1/4 cup	50 mL
Safflower oil (fatty acids)	1/2 cup	125 mL
Garlic oil (flavour, Ca. & potassium)	1 tbsp.	15 mL

Mix together in a suitable air tight container and store in the refrigerator. Give 1/4 tsp. for toy dogs, 1/2 - 1 tsp. for medium size dogs and up to 1 tbsp. for large dogs once a day with regular meal.

This formulation is limited in B and C vitamins as these vitamins are not fat or oil soluble. B's and C may be given by themselves or alternate the liquid supplement with the dry supplement. Use the liquid for several weeks then the dry for several weeks etc.

JOAN HARPER'S VITAMIN AND MINERAL MIX

Taken with permission from Joan Harper's Book, *The Healthy Cat and Dog Cook Book.*

All powders are mixed together:

Brewers yeast	2 cups	500 mL
Bone meal	1 cup	250 mL
Magnesium oxide powder	1/4 cup	50 mL
Alfalfa meal or powder	1/4 cup	50 mL
Tablespoons kelp	2 tbsp.	30 mL

Give 1/2 to 1 tablespoon per meal to your dog (average size)

Remember, we can overdo it on some vitamins, especially A and D and also the minerals calcium and phosphorus. Refer to the sections on pages 49, 51, and 60 to 69 for special precautions. Also, learn the nutrient contents of the various foods that contain these vitamins and minerals.

A Few Points When Feeding a Dog Naturally:

- use fresh and frozen ingredients vs canned
- use powders vs salts, example garlic powder vs garlic salt
- buy salt free butter
- make home made meat stocks vs bullion cubes (high salt)
- make home made soups vs prepared soups (additives and salt)
- use animal origin products vs plant sources: butter vs margarine
- bone meal or bone dust vs rock mineral
- raw vegetables can inhibit protein digestion
- cereals are better for fiber than vegetables and fruit
- dogs can only digest about 30 - 50 % of most vegetables due to their short intestines
- vegetable nutrients are hard for the dog to digest and therefore utilize
- use fresh vegetables and fruits
- for optimum effect, feed carotene and vitamin E together
- pectin and fiber helps for diarrhea and constipation
- egg has a Biological Value of 100, rice 75
- organ meats are the wild dogs first choice of the carcass
- cooking meats results in some breakdown of proteins
- dogs like aged foods
- fish is not a natural food source for dogs
- milk and some milk products have indigestible lactose
- cooking, heat, exposure to light and air can decrease or destroy some vitamins, especially water soluble vitamins

Yogurt

"the milk of eternal life"
Emperor Frances I of France

Yogurt is cultured milk that has been eaten for over 4000 years and is much easier to digest than milk. Yogurt has been credited with many health benefits over the years. It is a good protein source for dogs and is low in calories as well.

Joan Harper

This is a recipe for a complete dry dog food from Joan Harper's book: *The Healthy Cat and Dog Cookbook* *(copied with permission)*

Ground chicken necks and gizzards	**1 lb.**	**500 gm**
Chopped mackerel	**1 can**	**1 can**
Soybean flour (not defatted)	**2 cups**	**500 mL**
Wheat germ	**1 cup**	**250 mL**
Powdered skim milk	**1 cup**	**250 mL**
Cornmeal	**1 cup**	**250 mL**
Rye flour	**1 cup**	**250 mL**
Whole wheat flour	**2 cups**	**500 mL**
Bone meal (if not using neckbones)	**1 1/2 tbsp**	**23 mL**
Iodized sea salt or	**1 tbsp**	**15 mL**
Powdered kelp	**3 tbsp**	**45 mL**
Oil or Fat	**4 tbsp**	**60 mL**
Cod liver oil	**1 tbsp**	**15 mL**
Alfalfa powder	**1/4 cup**	**50 mL**
Garlic cloves, minced	**3**	**3**
Water	**4 cups**	**1 L**
Vitamin E	**400 IU**	**400 IU**
Brewers yeast	**1/2 cup**	**125 mL**

Mix ingredients to make a firm dough. Spread flat on a cookie sheet about 1/4 to 1/2 an inch thick. Bake in a moderate oven until golden brown for 1/2 to 3/4 of an hour. Cool and break into bite size chunks.

Sprinkle with 1/2 cup of brewers yeast and store in the refrigerator.

Protein 35% Fat 22% and Carbohydrate 43%

CHICKEN LIVER DELIGHT

A nutritious meal filled with vitamins and minerals.

Chicken livers, cut into small pieces	**8 - 10**	**8 - 10**
Rice	**1 1/2cup**	**375 mL**
Butter	**1/4 cup**	**50 mL**
Cheese, grated Parmesan	**1/2 cup**	**125 mL**

Cook rice as per direction on the box or using your own method. In a frying pan, melt the butter and cook the liver pieces for about 5 minutes stirring occasionally. When rice is cooked, stir in livers and sprinkle with garlic powder and cheese. Will serve a 30 lb (14 kg) dog 2 days.

SHRIMP SALAD

A tasty seafood salad, offering protein and vitamins A,D,B

Shrimp (frozen or canned)	**2 - 4 oz**	**55 - 125 g**
Cooked rice	**1 1/2 cups**	**375 mL**
Butter	**1/2 cup**	**125 mL**

Melt butter. Add shrimp to rice and stir. Blend in butter. Sprinkle (1/4 tsp.) sodium ascorbate powder, cool and serve. Serves a 10 lb (4.5 kg) dog 4 times.

SARDINE SALAD

Sardines, can	**1**	**1**
Cooked rice	**2 cups**	**500 mL**
Vegetable oil	**1/2 cup**	**125 mL**

Cook rice as directed. Mash up the sardines and oil and add to the hot rice. Cool, sprinkle with garlic powder. Serves a 20 lb (9 kg) dog 3 times.

Can be served hot on cold days and cool on hot days

Soup stock, chicken, or meat	**5 cups**	**1 L**
Carrots, scraped and finely		
chopped	**2**	**2**
Eggs	**4**	**4**
Cream	**1 cup**	**250 mL**
Flour	**2 tbsp.**	**30 mL**
Butter	**2 tbsp.**	**15 mL**

In a large saucepan, melt the butter and add flour making a smooth paste. Add stock slowly, avoiding lumps. Stir in carrots, bring to a boil stirring constantly. Reduce heat, cover and simmer until carrots are tender. Beat the eggs and cream in a small bowl and add to the soup. Cook another 5 minutes, stirring; do not let boil. Cool and serve. Serve warm or cool.

STEW & DUMPLINGS

Beef, flank, chuck or round	**1 lb**	**500 g**
Flour	**4 tbsp.**	**60 mL**
Butter	**2 tbsp.**	**30 mL**
Water	**2 cups**	**500 mL**
Potatoes, quartered	**2 cups**	**500 mL**
Carrots, cubes	**1 cup**	**250 mL**

Cut the meat into cubes depending on the size of the dog. Melt butter in sauce pan, roll meat in flour and brown. Add water and simmer for 30 minutes, add vegetables and cook another 30 minutes. Thicken gravy with rest of flour.

Flour	**1 cup**	**250 mL**
Baking powder	**2 tsp.**	**10 mL**
Salt	**1/4 tsp.**	**1 mL**
Butter	**1 tbsp.**	**15 mL**
Milk	**1/3 cup**	**75 mL**

Mix flour, baking powder and salt. Cut in butter. Stir in milk and drop from a tablespoon (15 mL) on top of stew. Cook 10 min. Serves a 30 lb (14 kg) dog 4 times. Add vitamin/minerals.

LAMB WITH RICE

Lamb and rice has become popular of late in commercial dog foods

Lamb, stewing or shoulder chops	2 lbs.	1 kg
Cooked rice	4 1/2 cups	1 L
Water	2 cups	500 mL
Butter	1 tbsp.	15 mL
Flour	2 tbsp.	30 mL
Kelp	1 tsp.	5 mL
Bone dust or bone meal	1 tsp.	5 mL
Vitamin C (sodium ascorbate)	1/2 tsp.	2 mL

Mix flour, kelp and bone meal. Cut lamb into small pieces and roll in flour mixture. Melt butter in frying pan, add meat and brown slightly. Add water, lamb and the rest of the flour mix to a casserole dish and bake at 350 F (180C) for about 45 minutes. Mix and serve with the rice. Will serve a 70 lb (32 kg) dog 3 times. Sprinkle the vitamin C (little less than 1/4 tsp. each)

FISH WITH MILK SAUCE

Thyme has lately been found to contain antioxidants.

Fish (remove all bones or used canned)	1 lb	1/2 kg
Boiling milk	1/2 cup	125 mL
Butter	1 tbsp.	15 mL
Flour	1 tbsp.	15 mL
Kelp	1 tsp.	5 mL
Thyme	1/4 tsp.	1 mL
Garlic powder	1/4 tsp.	1 mL

Cut the fish into bite size pieces and place in boiling milk. Simmer until well cooked. Make a sauce with the milk and other ingredients. Serve with the sauce to a 40 lb (18 kg) dog twice.

Who Left The Gate Open?

"Food and labor of feeding are the largest items of kennel expense"

    Mark Taynton, *Successful Kennel Management.*

We could call this section bulk or economical recipes. These are also recipes and ideas aimed at feeding a group of dogs.

Depending on circumstances such as availability of ingredients, help and time available, bulk feeding on our own may not be that economical. With many good commercial products on the market market today and a busy kennel schedule, time may be spent better in other areas such as cleanliness and facility repair, rather than mixing up and preparing meals. Storage also becomes a problem with bulk purchases. However, with a steady supply of ingredients at a reasonable cost with adequate and efficient means for preparation, bulk home kennel feeding can be economical.

The same rules apply regarding water, protein, fats, carbohydrates, vitamins and minerals. The only difference is that we are feeding more than one individual. All dogs are different, so feeding each individually and on a regular basis, as opposed to free choice, gives the kennel operator an opportunity to observe the eating habits of each dog. Adjustments can be made where necessary. Feeding large numbers of show dogs that may be owned by someone else puts great demands on the diet. Adequate nutrition is very important in these individuals if they are to look good and perform to the best of their ability. There are books on kennel management (page 249) that are for the kennel operator. These include feeding as well as other topics.

We can save on the purchase of ingredients. Purchasing in large quantities from butcher shops, feed mills and other food processors that may be in our area can save us money. As with all buying, buy wisely and consider storage facilities.

Those of us with just one or two dogs to feed also can save money.

Some Tips on Stretching Our Dog Food Budget.

- Ask neighbours and friends to save table-scraps.
  (Give them a covered container and guidelines on what
  to save and what not to save)
- Buy large volumes with friends and split (co-op style)
  - egg powder
  - whole wheat flour, rolled oats, rice and corn flour
  - bran, brewer yeast, macaroni and milk powders
  - Ascorbic acid or sodium ascorbate (vitamin C)
  - Alfalfa powder, bone meal, kelp powder and wheat
    germ
- Ask grocers and butchers for
  - off colour and over ripe vegetables and fruits
  - discoloured and freezer burnt meats and fish
  - stale and dry breads and buns (watch for mold)
  - out of date dairy products and eggs
  - damaged packages of cereals, flour or pancake mixes
  - off colour bulk items, cereals, pasta and flours
  - large bones, fat trim and bone dust

Stay away from sugar, (cakes, cookies) salt, (chips, tacos) and
damaged canned goods (Botulism)

BEAN CURD

*This bulk preparation rich in vitamin C, E and B complex as well
as fiber, protein and carbohydrate can go a long way. It can be
mixed with meat trimmings and fat drippings.*

Kidney beans, dry	**4 cups**	**2 Kg**
Water	**12 cups**	**2 1/2 L**

Soak the beans for at least 3 hours, then simmer for about 1 1/
2 hours. Boil for 30 minutes. Cool and use or store in refrigerator
to be used later in other recipes. 1/2 cup of the cooked beans
will provide a 60 lb. (27 kg) dog with adequate C and E and
about 15% B complex vitamins and 25% of his daily protein
requirements.

This recipe is an example of using our left-overs combined with some basic nutrition knowledge to produce 3 or 4 meals for our dog. With just the two of us and Turk, our Black Lab, at home, the amount of food eaten has lessened. Sandy, my wife took a chicken, removed the fat, skin, and deboned some of the meat. One meal we ate the drumsticks and thighs baked. For another meal, we had slices of the remaining chicken stir fried and added to a Caesar salad type dish. What was left (left-overs) was the fat, skin, and some bones.

Utilizing these chicken parts, some salad trimmings and some left-over sweet potato from the night before, I put together the following.

Chicken fat, skin, bones		
(from 1 chicken)	**1 cup**	**250 mL**
Salad trimmings		
(discoloured ends etc)	**1 cup**	**250 mL**
Kidney, beef		
(sliced into large chunks)	**1**	**1**
Water	**6 cups**	**1 1/2 L**
Oatmeal	**4 1/2 cups**	**1 L**
Sweet potato		
(left-over, sliced)	**1 cup**	**250 mL**
Kelp powder	**2 tbsp.**	**30 mL**

Put the first 4 ingredients into a large pot and simmer on low heat covered. After about 20 minutes add 1 cup of the oatmeal. Let simmer for 5 minutes, then stir and add another cup of oatmeal; add the sweet potato at this time. Continue to add more oatmeal and stir until all the oatmeal is added with the kelp last. Let cool, spoon out an amount reasonable for your dog and put the rest into an ice cream pail and save.

Nutritionally we have provided fat (chicken fat), protein (kidney), carbohydrate and fiber (oatmeal), vitamins and minerals (salad trimmings, potato, kelp, bones and kidney). We all can make recipes similar to this one.

BIG FAMILY DISH

A bulk recipe for a big eater or a group. Look out stand back.

Potatoes, sliced thin with skins, medium	6	6
Oat meal	2 cups	500 mL
Regular pork sausage	2 lbs	1 kg
Water	1/2 cup	125 mL
Garlic powder	1/2 tsp.	2 mL

Place the slices of potatoes and water on the bottom of a large roaster. Sprinkle the oat meal evenly on top of the potatoes. Separate the sausages and put on top evenly spaced. Sprinkle garlic powder last. Cover and bake in 300° F (150° C) for about 30 minutes. Cool, sprinkle with your choice of vitamin mineral mix (some recipes on page 150 of the Natural section) and serve portions depending upon the size of the dogs.

Provides carbohydrates, protein, fat, vitamins and minerals.

MACARONI HAMBURGER SALAD

A cool salad for those hot days of summer.

Macaroni (or pasta noodles)	2 cups	500 mL
Regular ground beef or pork	1 lb	1/2 kg
Water	2 cups	500 mL
Garlic cloves, finely chopped	1	1

Cook macaroni or pasta according to directions. Fry ground beef or pork. Drain macaroni and mix in meat including fat and chopped garlic. Cool and serve. 1 cup will serve a 30 lb (14 kg) dog his or her morning or evening meal. Vitamin and mineral mix can be sprinkled on top.

Treat biscuits or "bones"

Whole wheat flour	5 1/2 cups	1.25 L
Cracked wheat flour	3 cups	750 mL
Cornmeal	1 cup	250 mL
Milk powder	1/2 cup	125 mL
Yeast, envelope	1	1
Water, warm	1/4 cup	50 mL
Chicken or Beef broth	3 cups	750 mL
Egg, slightly beaten	1	1
Bone meal or Bone dust	4 tbsp.	60 mL
Garlic powder	1 tbsp.	15 mL

Mix the first 4 ingredients in a large bowel. Dissolve yeast in the water and add to the mixture. Add broth and form dough. Roll out about 1/4 in. (.5 cm) thick cut into "bones"; makes 30 large bones. Brush with egg glaze and bake at 300^0 F (150^0 C) for 45 min. Turn off oven and leave in oven over night to harden.

BULK RICE & CEREAL MIX

This mix can be made in large quantities and stored in the refrigerator and used either with left-overs or other recipes.
Since this is predominately carbohydrate, mixing with fat, protein, vitamins and minerals completes the meal.

Rice white or brown	2 cups	500 mL
Cereal grain (oats, barley or wheat)	1 cup	250 mL
Water or broth	3 cups	750 mL

In a large pot, mix the three and bring to a boil. Simmer for about 15 minutes. If using brown rice, use 3 times the simmering time. Cool and refrigerate for later use. Depending on the size of the dog, mix with the drippings from a roast and some protein such as cottage cheese, eggs, or meat scraps and a vitamin mineral supplement for a complete meal.

MEAT-VEGETABLE SOUP

Use our imagination and what we have available to make a soup that can be fed by itself or poured over dry dog food.

Raw soup bones	**2 - 3**	**2 - 3**
Water	**2 qts.**	**2 L**
Carrots, medium sized	**2**	**2**
Onion, small	**1**	**1**
Garlic powder	**1/2 tsp.**	**2 mL**

Put the bones and water into a large pot and bring to a boil. Reduce heat and simmer for 1 1/2 to 2 hours. Dice the carrots and onion and add to the soup. Cook for another 30 minutes. Sprinkle in the garlic powder, stirring as you add it. Remove the bones, cool and give to your dog, preferably outside to save the carpet. Feed the warm soup by itself or pour onto dry dog food or left-over rice, potatoes or other foods. Save the rest for later use. Many variations can be developed from this basic recipe using ingredients we have on hand.

Remember to heat up cold food right out of the refrigerator, for example, to "blood heat" temperature. This is just a term that is sometimes used which means body temperature. We wouldn't think of feeding a young baby milk straight out of the fridge without warming it up first. Warming up the food for the dog does several things:

- it is more "natural" for the carnivorous dog to eat warm food; however, the wild dogs do eat aged cairn.
- by warming food, the aromas produced stimulate appetite
- because dogs tend to gulp their food, the sudden shock of filling of the stomach with cold food may be upsetting.
- warm food should be easier to digest as chemical reactions of enzymes etc. require heat.

On hot days or after exercise, we may want to give cool foods, and the sudden lump of cold within the very core of the dog right next to the vital organs may be harmful.

BACON 'N' EGG PORRIDGE BREAKFAST

Pan fry this breakfast that will last all day.

Bacon, slices	3	3
Eggs	2	2
Porridge (oatmeal)	1 cup	250 mL
Milk	1/4 cup	50 mL
B complex 50mg tablet (crushed)	1	1
Vitamin C 250mg tablet (crushed)	1	1

Chop the bacon into 1/2 inch (cm) pieces and fry lightly in a pan. Add the porridge and continue until brown. Beat the eggs and milk in a small dish. Add the milk and well beaten eggs to the frying pan, stirring the while, as the eggs cook. Cool and sprinkle on the crushed vitamin tablets.

This is a powerful way to start the day with protein, energy and vitamins. Good for a 40 lb (18 kg) dog.

LEFTOVER OMELET

A good way to use leftover beef, chicken, turkey or pork.

Leftover meat	4-6 oz.	125-175 gm
Eggs	2	2
Oil	2 tbsp.	30 mL

Chop the meat scraps and fry in the oil. Beat the eggs gently and pour over the meat and continue frying.

Cool and cut into pieces, feed as is or mix with equal portions of dry dog food or rice or mashed potatoes. Can add a crushed multi-vitamin/mineral tablet or other vitamin/mineral supplement. Feed the amount that suits the size of dog.

DOGGIE SQUARES

We eat squares so here's some for our dogs.

Commercial Dog Chow	4 1/2 cups	1 L
Flour	1 cup	250 mL
Water	1 1/2 cups	374 mL
Eggs	2	2
Cooking oil	3 tbsp.	45 mL
Liver pate	3 tbsp.	45 mL

Mix flour, water, eggs and oil in a mixing bowel. Add dog chow and mix well. Put into an oiled 8/8 inch baking pan. Bake at 350° F (180°C) for about 45 minutes. Cool and spread liver pate on top as "icing". Cut into squares and enjoy.

Dry dog food can be put in a blender to make a meal of varying consistency depending on how long and how fast we run the blender. Add liquid if the nuggets are very hard.

Cooking is an art as well as a science. Trying a favorite recipe for our dog, with a few modifications for the reasons we have discussed, can be done by all of us. Commercial dog food can be used as an ingredient as we have done in several recipes, utilizing the texture and nutrient content accordingly. We may be surprised when we heat some dog foods, especially the poorer quality ones, for the unusual aromas that develop. Make your own judgements.

"It was so good, I don't feel an ounce of guilt".

Here we are going to be a little decadent and enjoy ourselves. With some recipes, we have thrown all caution to the wind. Fancy dishes can still be nutritious. For Birthdays, parties, Thanksgiving or Christmas, we over indulge once in a while; why can't our dog? Our dog can enjoy extra calories now and then; however, there are a few definite "no-no's". Our dog is our best friend, and we definitely don't want to hurt him. Foods to avoid and why

- chocolate: dogs are very sensitive to theobromine a compound in chocolate, which can cause vomiting, diarrhea, seizures and death. Four oz. of baking chocolate can poison a thirty pound dog.
- licorice is potassium binding
- "junk-food": high in sodium; the dog does not need salt
- candy and sweets: high in refined sugar, empty calories
- ice cream: lactose may be upsetting, causing diarrhea
- rhubarb: calcium binding, and the leaves are poisonous
- spicy foods can cause stomach irritations and upsets.

Just a few things to avoid and be aware of. Basically, what a dog likes are the flavours generally in fats. Over indulgence of fat can be upsetting and remember, fat has over twice the calories of other foods and may diminish appetite for other nutrients. Always remember our dog is a lot smaller than we are; a fifteen or twenty pound dog is one tenth our size. We are ten times bigger!

POLLACK SALAD

A seafood treat, rich in protein and vitamins D, E, B, and B_{12}.

Pollack	2 - 4 oz	55 - 125 g
Rice, cooked	1 1/2 cups	375 mL
Butter	1/2 cup	125 mL
Garlic powder	1/2 tsp.	2 mL

Melt butter. Add pollack to rice and stir. Blend in butter and sprinkle with garlic powder. Serves a 30 lb (14 kg) dog.

LAMB APRICOT PATTIES

Barbecue these apricot studded lamb patties and serve with yogurt sauce. According to nutritionists, the richest and most nourishing fruit is the dried apricot. As well as being a source of energy, it contains vitamin A, E, calcium, phosphorus, iron, and potassium.

Lamb, lean ground	1 lb	500 g
Bread crumbs, fine dry	1/2 cup	125 mL
Egg	1	1
Apricots, dried, **finely chopped**	1/3 cup	75 mL
Yogurt, plain	4 tbsp.	60 mL

Combine the ground lamb, bread crumbs, egg and apricots. Divide into 4 equal sized portions and shape each into a patty about 1/2 to 3/4 in. (1-2cm) thick. Barbecue for about 5 minutes on each side and let cool. Serve with a tablespoon of yogurt topping. 1 patty serves a 25 lb (11 kg) dog. Save the rest.

DEEP FRIED CHICKEN GIZZARDS OR LIVERS

A tasty, nutritious canine delicacy.

Chicken gizzards or livers	1 lb	500 g
Whole wheat flour	1 1/3 cup	325 mL
Butter, melted	1 tbsp.	15 mL
Egg yolks, beaten	2	2
Egg whites, stiffly beaten	2	2

In a medium size bowl, mix the flour, butter and egg yolks. Cover the rest and put in the refrigerator for 3 to 12 hours. If feeding a small dog, cut the gizzards in half. Just before use, add egg whites and gizzards or livers. Fry in deep fat, heated to 365^0 F (185^0 C) until reasonably brown. Cool and give as treats; save the rest.

A Christmas treat using turkey leftovers.

Cream of chicken soup	10 oz	284 mL
Water	1/4 cup	50 mL
Chow mein noodles	1 cup	250 mL
Turkey (chopped)	1 cup	250 mL
Garlic powder	1/4 tsp.	1 mL

Place soup, water, noodles, and turkey into a 1 1/2 - quart casserole. Stir and sprinkle garlic powder on top. Bake for 45 minutes in a 375^0 F (190^0 C) oven. Cool and serve.
Serves a 70 lb (32 kg) dog.

TURKEY CRISP

This is a delicious turkey variation.

Turkey (chopped)	1 cup	250 mL
Oatmeal	1 cup	250 mL
Vegetable oil	2 tbsp.	30 mL
Dry onion soup mix	1 1/2 oz	45 g
Vitamin C, 250 mg		
crushed tablet	1	1

Warm the turkey with the oil in a medium sized pan. Mix in the oatmeal and continue frying for a minute, stirring continuously.
Finally, add the onion soup mix, still stirring. Cool, stir in the vitamin C and serve. Vitamin C is susceptible to loss by heat or exposure to air, so we always add it last to keep its potency.
Serves a 30 lb (14 kg) dog.

PIERRE'S HAM, PEA SOUP

Ham bone	1	1
Split peas	1 cup	250 mL
Water	10 cups	2.75 L
Garlic cloves (crushed)	3	3
Butter	2 tbsp.	30 mL

In a large pot, simmer the ham bone and water for about 1 hour. Remove the bone (give to dog, preferably outside). In a saucepan melt butter, add crushed garlic, the split peas and cook for about 5 minutes. Add this to the liquid from the ham bone and let simmer for about 2 hours. Let cool for 15 minutes, then puree the mixture in a blender. Serve warm, portion depending upon the size of the dog. Save the rest to serve by itself or in combination with dry dog food or other recipes.

YOGURT, CHICKEN & BARLEY SOUP

Excellent on cold winter days

Chicken cooked, shredded	2 oz	55 g
Pearl barley	1/2 cup	125 mL
Chicken stock	5 cups	1.25 L
Yogurt, plain	2 cups	500 mL
Butter	2 tbsp.	30 mL
Bone dust or bone meal	2 tbsp.	30 mL
Brewers yeast	2 tbsp.	30 mL
Vitamin C (500 mg crushed tablet)	1	1

Melt butter in a large saucepan, add chicken stock and bring to a boil. Reduce heat, add barley and simmer for 50 minutes. Add shredded chicken and simmer another 10 minutes. Beat yogurt and add to the soup. Add last three ingredients at this time. Serves two 30 lb (14 kg) dogs.

APRICOT-APPLE-ORANGE RELISH

A nutritious fruit relish, used as a sweet topping.

Apricots, dried, chopped	**1 lb**	**500 g**
Apples, green, peeled,		
** cored, sliced**	**2**	**2**
Oranges, sliced	**2**	**2**
Garlic cloves	**3**	**3**
Water	**1 cup**	**250 mL**
Vitamin C (1000mg)		
** crushed or powder**	**1000 mg**	**1 g**
Vitamin B complex		
** crushed tablets**	**2**	**2**
Wheat germ (vitamin E)	**4 tbsp.**	**60 mL**

In a large pot, put the first five items and bring to a boil. Reduce heat and simmer gently uncovered for about 4 hours. Stir often during the last hour and add the last 3 ingredients stirring in well. (vitamin C and B's will be lost by cooking so add last) Serve as a relish on meat dishes or on dry dog food.

TONGUE-RICE CASSEROLE

An "unspeakable" casserole.

Beef Tongue, sliced	**2 lbs.**	**1 kg**
Rice, partly cooked		
** or left-over**	**3 cups**	**750 mL**
Fat drippings,		
** or melted butter**	**1/4 cup**	**50 mL**
Tomato juice	**4 1/2 cups**	**1 L**
Garlic powder	**2 tbsp.**	**30 mL**

Simmer tongue with fat drippings or butter for about 30 minutes. Transfer to a roaster or casserole dish and stir in rice and tomato juice. Sprinkle with garlic powder. Bake in 350⁰ F (180⁰ C) for 30 minutes. Serves a 30 lb (14 kg) dog up to 4 times. Serving amounts vary with the dog and activity.

BIRTHDAY CAKE

Be sure to sing Happy Birthday before serving this cake.

Cake flour	1 cup	250 mL
Baking powder	1 1/2 tsp.	7 mL
Garlic powder	1/4 tsp.	1 mL
Shortening, softened	1/4 cup	50 mL
Sugar (required in a cake recipe)	1/2 cup	125 mL
Egg	1	1
Milk	1/2 cup	125 mL
Liver pate (for "icing)	3 tbsp.	45 mL

Sift flour and measure. Resift with baking and garlic powder. In a mixing bowl, beat shortening until creamy. Add sugar gradually, beating well. Add egg and beat until the creamed mixture is light and fluffy. Add milk, alternating with the flour mixture, to the shortening mixture one-third at a time, ending with the flour. Stir after each addition until the mixture is smooth. Place in a 10 X 15 in. (25 X 38 cm, 1.2 L) pan or 6 greased muffin tins. Bake at 350⁰ F (180⁰ C) for about 25 to 30 minutes. Cool and "ice" with liver pate. Cut into 6 equal parts.

FRUIT PIE

Unflavored gelatin	1 packet	1 packet
Water, cold	2 tbsp.	30 mL
Water, boiling	1/2 cup	125 mL
Yogurt, plain	1 cup	250 mL
Fruit, small chunks, your choice	3/4 cup	175 mL
Graham cracker crust (see page 173)	1	1

Sprinkle gelatin over cold water in a medium mixing bowl; let stand 5 minutes. Add boiling water and dissolve gelatin. Beat in yogurt and refrigerate for about 45 minutes. Fold in fruit and pour into pie crust. Refrigerate for about 4 hours.
Serves four: 30 lb (14 kg) party dogs.

GRAHAM CRACKER PIE CRUST

A tasty pie crust that can be used with fillings of our choice.

Graham wafer crumbs	3/4 cup	175 mL
Butter, melted	4 tbsp.	60 mL
Garlic powder	1/4 tsp.	1 mL

Combine all ingredients and press into a pie plate or cake pan. Chill in refrigerator for 2 hours before filling.

GOURMET DRINKS

RED "WINE" CANINE STYLE

After roasting beef, lamb or pork, remove the roast and half fill the roaster with water. Warm for several minutes and add a sprinkle of garlic powder. Stir and scrape the roaster bottom to lift off any meat. Pour into a container to be used as a cold or warm drink later.

DINGO-AID

A drink that will quench the thirst on a hot day or after vigorous exercise.

Water	9 cups	2 L
Lite salt (potassium chloride)	2 tbsp.	30 mL
Vitamin C (powder or crushed tablet)	500 mg	500 mg
Vitamin B complex 50 mg crushed tablet	3	3

Crush the tablets well and dissolve in the water. Serve cold.

POPSICLES

Something to lick on those hot days of summer. Using either of the top two recipes, pour the liquid into ice cube containers or popsicle molds and freeze. Once frozen, remove from container and store in a plastic bag for later use. Can be put into empty food dish for a cool refreshment.

ROYAL GOURMET PANCAKES

Pancakes fit for a King or Queen, even a Prince or Princess.

Potatoes, peeled		
(about 3 medium)	**1 lbs**	**1/2 kg**
Flour	**1 tbsp.**	**15 mL**
Eggs	**1**	**1**
Milk or Cream	**1/2 cup**	**125 mL**
Garlic powder	**1/4 tsp.**	**1 mL**
Bacon strips		
(or other meat chopped)	**2**	**2**
Relish (page 171 optional)	**3 tbsp.**	**45 mL**

Cut potatoes into reasonable size chunks and blend in blender with the other 4 ingredients. Chop bacon or meat into small pieces and add after blending. Pour onto hot greased frying pan an amount suitable for the size of the dog. Turn and fry on the other side. Fry all of the batter and save for later if dog is small. Cool, spread relish over pancake and serve.
Serve to your Royal Highness. Tut, tut no sampling.

BREAD RAISIN PUDDING

A delicious dessert.

Dry bread cubes	**1 cup**	**250 mL**
Egg, slightly beaten	**2**	**2**
Milk, hot	**1 cup**	**250 mL**
Garlic powder	**1/4 tsp.**	**1 mL**
Raisins	**1/2 cup**	**125 mL**
Butter	**1 tbsp.**	**15 mL**

Put bread in a buttered baking dish. Mix the next 3 ingredients and pour over the bread. Add raisins and dot with butter. Set dish in a shallow pan of hot water. Bake at 300⁰ F (150⁰ C) until browned, about 30 - 45 minutes. Will serve a 30 lb (14 kg) dog 4 times.

In this section of recipes, we shall discuss the feeding of dogs with special requirements. Until now we have presented recipes for dogs requiring the maintenance levels of nutrients. The following are for special case individuals.

Separately we shall cover the feeding of the

- Overweight Dog
- Underweight Dog
- Sick and Convalescing Dog and Puppy
- Mother Dog
- Puppy
- Orphan Puppy
- Neutered Individual
- Working Active Dog

Adjustments are made for these individuals as their requirement levels for the various nutrients are different than for the dog on a maintenance diet. Each special situation will be covered from a nutritional stand point, followed by some recipes.

Some of these special case dogs are under a common term we call stress. It is appropriate to discuss stress at this time. Stress is involved in such things as illness, surgery, whelping, nursing, growing or working. Other things like travel, fear, and lack of accustomed affection are also stressful. It is important to know how the dog responds to stress and how we can help.

What is stress? Stress is a demand that is put on our dog. The internal systems go on the alert, nerves tingle and hormones pump into the blood stream causing heartbeat and breathing rates to increase and muscles to tense. Extra energy and protein is needed to repair cells, produce antibodies and make new red blood cells. Extra vitamins and minerals also become important to furnish the added requirements to cope with the stress.

A certain amount of stress is healthy; however, problems start when the stress becomes continuous. Constant demands, pressures and uncertainties draw on reserves of nutrients and body cells. If the stress is more than the dog can handle, changes become apparent. Increased susceptibility to disease, premature aging and behavioral changes can result. If our dog is suffering from too much stress, whatever the source, he or she will be depressed, inactive and unresponsive - the typical "burn out" syndrome.

The amount of stress our dog can tolerate will depend upon his or her general health, nutrition, breed personality and owner support and caring. Some breeds and certain individuals thrive on action and are capable of coping with more stress.

Quality protein, fat, vitamins and minerals become important in the diet, fat, for concentrated fuel, and the amino acids of protein for tissue maintenance. Animal proteins and fats serve best here in a balance with all the other nutrients.

We have to help our dog to manage stress by identifying it and giving him or her assistance to deal with it. We can start by reducing the stressful environment and giving as much comfort as possible. Regular feeding of a nutritious diet, with fresh water and a quiet place to rest is half the battle. Attention and affection can help lessen their burden. When in doubt, we can think like a dog and image ourselves in the situation.

Routine vaccinations and treatment for internal and external parasites, when present, must be part of the health regime. Visits to the veterinarian for examinations and consultation are important in preventing and avoiding emergencies. Our primary aim is the health and well-being of our dog.

" A fat dog is not a healthy dog, but a badly fed dog."
    Jean Powell

*"Obesity is a preventable disease, and it's up to you to
    prevent it! "*
    Dr. Jane R. Bicks DVM

Obesity is the increase in body weight beyond the limitations of skeletal and physical requirements. This increase is due to an excessive accumulation of body fat. The mass of fat is more than twenty percent of the total body mass.

Obesity is the number one disease problem in our pets today. There are more fat dogs today then ever before, and the numbers are increasing every day. The primary problem is too many calories and not enough activity. Overweight dogs go on to have other problems caused by carrying this excess "baggage".

Problems arising from Obesity:

- life expectancy is greatly shortened
- more veterinary medical costs
- greater susceptibility to disease and injury
- increased anesthetic and surgical risk
- longer to recover after surgery or illness
- poor wound healing
- lower fertility, difficult whelping and poor lactation
- contributes to nutritional deficiencies
- increased pressure on internal organs
- increased blood pressure
- contributing factor to heart, lung and skeletal problems
- shortness of breath and greater risk of heat stroke
- increased risk of diabetes, liver and kidney problems
- decreased ability to exercise and play

There is no question a lean dog is far healthier and will live longer. Obesity does, however, reduce the risk of osteoporosis and increases a dog's tolerance to cold weather.

Causes of Obesity:

- consuming more calories than required due to
  - convenience of high quality commercial dog food
  - table scraps high in fat
  - being fed by the neighbours
  - being fed snacks between meals
  - giving food instead of love and attention
  - boredom
  - not using a maintenance diet but a puppy or stress diet

- obese puppy, early production of large numbers of fat cells
- neutering, decreases hormones and resulting activity
- pregnancy, consuming more in preparation for lactation
- lack of exercise
- advancing age with less activity
- congestive heart failure, hypothyroidism, diabetes mellitus
- breeds: labs, terriers, spaniels, dachshunds, beagles

Dogs require energy for the basic body functions and activities. Any extra is saved as body fat for the day when they may be short of energy. In the wild, where hunting and scavenging are the means of getting food, saving for the days when food may be in short supply is important. Feast and famine are in a constant cycle. Our domestic dog gets to feast everyday but continues to prepare for famine. We must reduce the feast and add a little famine.

How can we tell if our dog is overweight? We can assess our dog by weighing and comparing to others of the same age and breed, or we can do a physical examination. Ribs should not be visible but be easily felt. We should feel a light cover of fat under the skin. When looked down from above the dog, his rib cage should be wider than his abdomen, forming an "hourglass figure" and the stomach should be tucked up, not loose and flabby. If his weight is over the breed average and we can't feel the ribs, we have an obese dog.

Prevention is the best medicine. However, if our dog is a little "fat", what should we do? First, we must determine the cause. If we have eliminated any medical problem and too many calories is the cause, reducing the number of calories is the treatment.

Our objective is to promote a loss of body fat while conserving lean muscle tissue. When we put our dog on a reducing diet, we must remember this. We want the dog to lose body fat but not affect the other tissues like muscles and bones. There are commercially prepared reducing diets on the market today that are primarily low calorie and high fiber. Indigestible fiber levels of fifteen to twenty-five percent give the dog of feeling of satisfaction because he has something in his stomach that does not supply any nutrients. The fat content is less than nine percent as well. Protein, vitamins and minerals are kept at the regular amounts so that muscle and bone tissue are not affected by the diet. The goal is to reduce the number of calories without affecting intake.

How to Lose Weight?

- make a commitment and set a weight goal
- monitor weight loss and body condition regularly
- feed less and more often, twenty to thirty percent less
- don't forget protein, vitamins and minerals
- create good eating habits, feed regularly and on time
- avoid fat and high calorie foods
- give love and attention instead of snacks
- substitute vegetables for high calorie snacks
- give attention to behavioral changes
- have only one person in charge of feeding
- increase exercise and play
- try to eliminate boredom with toys or other pets
- if a house pet, keep room cooler
- if two or more dogs, separate at feeding
- commercial reducing diets require the same commitments
- be firm and don't give in

Remember this is all in the dog's best interest. Obesity is detrimental to the dog's health and life expectancy.

Dieting need not be severe. What is required is an awareness of the problems and the benefits of the final results.

Overweight and Obesity: (Warrants repeating)

- most important problem of our pets today
- have medical conditions attended to
- obesity shortens life span and increases medical problems
- obesity is carried from puppyhood to adulthood
- reducing requires commitment and firmness
- feed less of regular food or try reducing preparations
- utilize indigestible fiber to decrease hunger
- increasing fiber content may hinder absorption of nutrients
- body fat as well as muscle may be lost when reducing
- exercise, burning more calories, is part of the program
- prevention by providing only enough calories to maintain a normal body weight

LOW FAT HIGH FIBER

Balanced for protein, vitamins and mineral. Low in calories and high in fiber.

Beef lean ground	**4 oz**	**125 g**
Cottage Cheese dry	**1/2 cup**	**125 mL**
Carrots cooked	**2 cups**	**500 mL**
Green Beans cooked	**2 cups**	**500 mL**
Bone meal	**1 tsp.**	**5 mL**
Garlic powder	**1/2 tsp.**	**2 mL**

Cook beef, drain fat. Mix in other ingredients. Sprinkle with garlic. Feeds 1, 30 - 40 lb (14 - 18 kg) dog one day

Utilizes vegetables to provide fiber and bulk. Low fat dairy products supply protein, vitamins and minerals while reducing calories.

Tasty low calorie, high fiber reducing recipe.

Beef Tongue diced	1 lb	500 g
Carrots sliced	2	2
Celery stalks, with leaves chopped	2	2
Tomato juice, low sodium	1 cup	250 mL
Water	1 cup	250 mL
Bone meal	1 tsp.	5 mL
Corn starch	2 tsp.	10 mL
Parsley chopped	3 tsp.	15 mL

Mix first six ingredients in large sauce pan and simmer for 1 hour. Mix cornstarch with 2 tbsp. water and add slowly to tongue mixture. Stir and cook until thickened. Add parsley and cool.

Feeds 30 - 40 lb (14 - 18 kg) dog 2 days

MEAT LOAF

Beef lean ground	1 1/2 lbs.	700 g
Egg beaten	1	1
Water	3/4 cup	175 mL
Rolled oats	1 cup	250 mL
Brewers yeast	1 tbsp.	15 mL
Bone meal	1 tsp.	5 mL
Kelp	1 tsp.	5 mL
Garlic powder	1/2 tsp.	2 mL
Grated Cheddar cheese	1/2 cup	125 mL

Put first 8 ingredients into large bowl. Mix together well. Pack into a loaf pan 9 x 5 x 3 inches (23 x 12 x 7 cm).
Bake uncovered in 350° F (180° C) oven of 1 hour.

Spread grated cheese over meat and return to oven to melt. Cool, serves 30 - 40 lb (14 - 18 kg) dog 4 days.

Underweight

Be sure the dog is actually underweight. Is our dog in poor body condition for his or her age, breed and level of activity? Can we see the ribs and hips readily and does the dog seem listless? Have the dog examined for illness, infectious disease or the presence of internal parasites. If an intact female, she may be pregnant. Talk to other owners of the same breed of dog and ask about the breed characteristics.

Some dogs, by nature, are, "hard keepers". Get a professional opinion on the dog's condition as health and well-being are what is important not external appearances. Fit dogs are not fat.

Having done all this and we believe that our dog should have a little more "fat on his bones", then a diet with a increase in caloric intake or an examination of the feeding routine may be appropriate.

The dog may be a fussy eater. Fussy eaters are made, not born.

A few hints for these type of individuals:

- develop a feeding routine, feed at the same time every day
- if limited feeding, try free choice
- develop an exercise and play schedule to improve appetite.
- all dogs are individuals, some need company or activity going on for them to eat.
- or feed in a quiet place where the dog is not disturbed
- try wholesome meal snacks
- change the diet, try fresh food, such as raw meat, or liver
- warm and/or moisten the meal
- try table scraps, especially fat drippings
- we might try a puppy or performance type dog food which has more protein and energy in the ingredients.
- always have water available

Refer to the gourmet section, page 167 for high calorie recipes.

There is a harmony that is seen in the dog's body with the many complex interactions of all body functions playing all in tune to the same symphony. When the dog is sick, for whatever reason, the harmony is "out of tune" and healing is the body's way of getting back in tune.

Feeding the sick during illness or while convalescing after surgery deserves special attention. By nature a dog will lose it's appetite and not eat when it is sick or distressed. This is nature's way of trying to "heal thyself". By not eating, the dog is giving its digestive system a rest so that all the body systems can concentrate on getting better. Loss of appetite is a good indicator of a digestive problem or poor health, and a return to eating is a sign that things are improving.

With diminished appetite and a reduction in food intake, there may be a decrease in protein, the essential nutrient for the repair and building of tissues. Other nutrients such as energy, vitamins and minerals may also be reduced.

Some conditions, such as a sore throat or a plugged nose, may also add to what appears to be a lack of appetite. Offering warm, moist, soft food and cleaning the nostrils may help.

The primary aim in feeding the sick is to give easily digested, highly concentrated, nutrient rich foods, especially protein. Since the amount of food ingested will be small, we should insure that what is eaten will be useful.

Oral medications given during illness often disrupt the digestive system, resulting in abdominal discomfort and diarrhea with loss of nutrients and fluids. This places more importance on replacing those nutrients and watching for dehydration. Water should always be available.

MOM'S CHICKEN SOUP

Good for us and good for dogs

Chicken noodle soup package	1	1
Water half as much called for		
Butter melted	**1 tbsp.**	**15 mL**
Brewers yeast	**1 tsp.**	**5 mL**
Vitamins infant liquid	**6 drops**	**.5 mL**
Vitamin C tablet crushed, or powder	**250 mg**	**250 mg**
Garlic powder	**1 tsp.**	**5 mL**

Heat the soup mix as directed on the package only with 1/2 the amount of water. When ready, add the other ingredients. Cool and serve warm.

HOSPITAL PORRIDGE

Easily digested, high protein, and fortified.

Farina (Cream of Wheat ®) cooked to make 2 cups	**1/2 cup**	**125 mL**
Cottage cheese creamed	**1 1/2 cup**	**375 mL**
Egg	**1**	**1**
Brewer's yeast	**2 tbsp.**	**30 mL**
Butter melted	**2 tbsp.**	**30 mL**
Bone meal	**1 tsp.**	**5 mL**
Vitamin C (tablet crushed) or powder	**250 mg**	**250 mg**
Vitamins infant liquid (or 1 adult multi-vitamin tablet crushed)	**10 drops**	

Cook farina according to directions. Mix in other ingredients. Cool and serve warm.

Will feed a 30 - 40 lb (14 - 18 kg) dog one day.

Good every day supplement or meal for convalescing dogs with poor appetites, or dogs with skin problems. Liver contains a high concentration of vitamins and minerals as well as being very palatable.

Chicken livers	1 lb.	.5 kg
Corn oil	1/2 cup	125 mL
Bran	4 cups	1 L
Bone meal	1/2 tsp.	2 mL

Blend all ingredients. Put into ice cube tray or into muffin tin with cups. Use ice cube trays for small dogs and muffins for large dogs. Freeze. Can remove from trays and store in large plastic bag frozen. Warm and feed one per day.

Highly nutritious and tasty

Yogurt plain (not low fat)	1 cup	500 g
Honey warmed or liquid	3 tbsp.	45 mL
Vitamin C tablet crushed	250 mg	250 mg
B complex adult tablet crushed	1	1

Add honey to yogurt and warm in Microwave or on stove. Mix in vitamins and serve warm.

A recipe high in protein, energy and vitamins.

To feed the sick and convalescing dog use ingredients that are highly palatable, easily digested and rich in nutrients. Serving the food warm makes it easier for the dog to smell the aromas and improve his appetite. Foods rich in protein and fat supply nutrients for building, repair of tissues and concentrated energy.

MOTHERS

A bitch well-nourished during gestation and properly fed during lactation will be able to provide for her puppies for the first three weeks of their lives. Bitches bred at optimal weight should return to optimal weight by weaning.

When the bitch has been properly nourished, breeding and conception conditions are optimal. Poor nutrition may result in low conception rates, fetal abnormalities and mammary gland changes affecting the quality and quantity of milk. Poor quality feeding of a pregnant mother can cause loss of body weight. Uncontrolled diarrhea from poorly digested low quality food may happen. Weak and dead puppies, no milk, or little milk and anemia may also develop. Feeding a diet that is balanced for her condition in sufficient quantity that she can digest should begin early in her reproductive career and doesn't end until the puppies are weaned. Her ration should have at least 1600 digestible calories per pound of food at this time.

The standard maintenance diets for adult dogs do not have the required amounts for protein, energy, vitamins and minerals, so just giving more of this type of ration is not enough. A puppy growing formula is more appropriate to the gestation/lactation requirements. A gestation/lactation formula dog food having: twenty-nine percent protein or more, seventeen percent fat or more, less than five percent fiber, calcium 1 - 1.8%, and phosphorus .8 - 1.6 % on a dry matter basis is essential. These are the same for the growing puppy, so the whole family can eventually eat together. This level is particularly important during the last three to four weeks before whelping and the first three weeks of lactation. Find a good quality dog food that meets these requirements, balanced with vitamins and minerals. Additional supplementation is not necessary. Feeding a poor quality dog food and supplementing in hopes of improving the formulation will only make matters worse.

Excessive supplementing with few exceptions may induce problems. Excess calcium and phosphorus, for example, may lead to tissue calcification and abnormalities in the puppies. In turn, a diet with a lot of meat and no bones can lead to calcium deficiency.

During gestation it is not uncommon for bitches to have two periods when they may lose their appetite, first around the fourth to fifth week of gestation and just before whelping. This is due to hormonal changes at these times. If this loss of appetite lasts longer than forty-eight hours, a medical examination should be made.

Approximately one third of the fetal growth happens in the first five weeks of gestation and no change in the mother's weight will be evident. The rest of the growth occurs in the last four weeks with her weight increasing by fifteen to twenty-five percent. This being the case, she can be fed the same amount as she normally would have but gradually increased by fifteen to twenty-five percent more by the time she whelps. As she is gaining weight, she should be fed at least twice a day or free choice. She is physically limited in how much she can consume at one time because of the presence of the enlarging puppies in her abdomen. We also can moisten her food at this time to increase her water intake. Always have free access to good water.

Whelping Tips

- use a large sturdy whelping box with a cover
- use towels or carpeting that can be washed for flooring
- cleanliness is very important
- do not interfere unless necessary
- if she has not removed the placenta from the puppy soon after birth, we must, thus allowing them to breath
- be sure all after birth, placenta, has been expelled
- a reddish brown discharge usually means all after births have been expelled
- any other colour, brown or greenish, up to forty-eight hours later may mean that afterbirth, uterine infection or another puppy is retained.

Once the puppies are born and lactation begins, we must increase the amount fed. The bitch must be given enough energy so that she can produce sufficient milk to meet the needs of the nursing puppies. In large breeds with big litters, this can be as much as two liters (one half gallon) per day. If the intake is not adequate, she will take from her own body stores and production levels will drop. The first week she should be fed at least one and a half times the amount she would get before breeding, twice as much for the second week and triple in the third week. These amounts are a guideline and will depend upon the size of the litter. Weighing the puppies regularly can help to monitor their progress. Feed the bitch or supplement accordingly.

Free choice feeding or meal feeding at least three times a day insures that she gets all she wants and also encourages the puppies to start eating solid food. Some breeders of small breed dogs use a good quality growth/lactation formulated cat food as these cat foods have higher nutrient and energy contents.

Caloric density, the concentration of calories, must be high in the diet for the lactating bitch in that she has to eat, digest, absorb, and use large amounts of nutrients to produce large quantities of milk. As her stomach and digestive system are only so big, the concentration of energy in the diet must be high. This is why the protein and fat content of gestation/ lactation is so high. To increase this density, we might give added fat. One tablespoon (15 ml) of fat/cup of dry food. Butter, lard, tallow, bacon fat or vegetable oil are all suitable. Doing this will bring up the caloric density by twenty-five to thirty percent. Greater than this may cause her to cut back on total intake, jeopardizing her intake of other nutrients such as protein, vitamins and minerals.

Supplementing the bitch with the water soluble vitamins: beta carotene, B complex and vitamin C, can be done with little danger; however, the fat soluble vitamins A and D can be overdone. Vitamin E excess is not believed to be as critical.

We can start decreasing the mother's food after three weeks as the puppies are beginning to eat solid food on up to six weeks when they will be weaned. This gradual decrease of food intake has her producing less milk as the puppies are becoming less and less dependent on her. During full lactation she should be up to three times the amount she would get before she was bred. On the day of weaning the following procedure will help her "dry-up".

- 1st. day no food and all the water she would like
- 2nd. day 1/4 of her regular maintenance amount
- 3rd. day 1/2 of her regular amount
- 4th. day 3/4 of her regular amount
- 5th. day feed her her normal pre-pregnancy amount

Start changing over to an adult maintenance food and off the gestation/lactation ration unless she is down in condition. This changeover is done over several days by mixing the two foods together so as not to upset her. (Some breeders will also limit water intake to two small drinks a day at this time. Limiting water should be done with care, so she does not become too dehydrated.)

Summary

- the better condition the mother is in, the better chance the puppies have
- provide a quality diet, balanced for gestation/lactation
- high caloric density is essential
- caution is needed when adding minerals, especially calcium and phosphorus
- whelping is a natural phenomena that has been done for millions of years
- monitor the weight of the puppies regularly, preferably daily, for signs of poor growth
- supplement puppies' if necessary
- increase the amount fed and frequency of feeding or allow free choice
- start puppies on solid food after the second or third week
- start preparing for weaning after the third week
- make weaning a smooth transition for mother and puppies
- enjoy and take satisfaction in a job well done

PUPPIES

Growing puppies are very vulnerable to an improper diet. Most dogs will have completed their physical growth by the time they are nine months old, which is one twentieth of the time required by humans. If the puppies have been properly feed during their youth, there is little, under normal circumstances, that can harm them later as adults.

The demands for growth are great and, if they are not met, a dog will not reach its genetic potential. If this potential growth is not reached, it can never be regained. On the other hand, a dog cannot be fed so that it exceeds its genetic potential. The growth of the puppy starts with the dam at conception. Her proper nourishment begins the process that continues on after birth until weaning. Proper nutrition is essential.

As soon as possible after the birth the puppies will start nursing. This first milk, colostrum, is important as it provides immunity which will protect the puppies against infectious disease until they produce their own immunity. Colostrum is rich is antibodies that the mother's immune system has made from her various vaccinations and exposures to disease organisms during her life. In dogs, very few of these antibodies are passed through the placenta making the first suck of colostrum very important.

Initially the puppies will only eat and sleep. Their eyes and ears open around ten to sixteen days and fifteen to seventeen days respectfully. During this time they should be gaining weight and have normal stools. If the mother is short of milk, for what ever reason, refer to the section on orphan puppies (195) for supplementing.

As well as supplemental feeding, the mother should have a medical examination by a veterinarian to diagnose and treat any medical problem that may be the cause of poor milk production. Barring this, she may not be getting adequate nourishment herself. Refer to the section on lactating mothers for guidelines.

Puppies that are hungry will cry and be restless whereas well-fed puppies will be contented and gain weight. A puppy should gain about one to two grams/day/lb of the expected adult weight for the breed. A puppy who will weight thirty pounds as an adult should gain thirty to sixty grams (one to two oz) per day for the first five to six months. Weighing the puppies will give a good indication if they are growing to their potential and the mother is feeding them adequately. Puppies will lose ten percent of their weight in the first twenty to forty-eight hours after birth and from then on should gain everyday. If this general goal is not being met, supplemental feeding is in order. Some breeders alternate bottle feeding half the litter every day so that all puppies get a chance to nurse. The rapid rate of growth is continued for six to nine months. Giant breeds take longer, eighteen months to two years, for the growing to level off.

Overfeeding, on the other hand, can be detrimental. "Roly-poly" little "butter balls" will have problems later on. Overfeeding, supplying a greater intake of calories than protein, can result in disproportionate growth for the puppy. Their body systems grow from protein, building nervous, skeletal, and muscular tissue. Carbohydrate or fat calories are used for energy, and extra is saved as body fat. The result is fat, plump puppies that are not developing the muscles and bones as they should. Overfeeding calories develops many more fat cells that will predispose to obesity in adulthood. This extra weight also puts added stress on the soft, growing bones and joints. It has been shown that it is better to slightly under feed, in that growth will be even for all systems and the dogs will live longer with fewer problems. The best opinions of the day advise that a controlled intake of quality puppy food fed two to three times a day, as opposed to free choice, is best for growth and the prevention of obesity and skeletal problems.

Puppy nutrition is critical for adequate protein, vitamins and minerals as well as the correct balance of energy.

When purchasing a commercially prepared dogfood for the puppies, look for a high quality growth puppy food. The label should show at least twenty-nine percent protein, seventeen percent fat, less than five percent fiber, 1.0 - 1.8 calcium, 0.8 - 1.6 phosphorus and eighty percent digestible. If the company has done feeding trials, so much the better. These high quality foods are balanced and when fed in the correct amounts, will supply all the nutritional requirements for all breeds of dogs. Additional supplementation, especially the minerals calcium and phosphorus, have been shown in many studies to be detrimental. Many dog foods contain more than the NRC recommendations for calcium and phosphorus, so we do not have to worry or supply extra. If we are still unsure, consult with our veterinarian, dog nutritionist or contact the quality dog food manufacturers for more information.

If we are to prepare our own home formulated recipes for growing puppies, beware that this is a critical period in their lives and slight miscalculations can be disastrous. Much time and money has been spent in research on this topic so we should take full advantage of it. Replacing no more than twenty percent of the diet with home recipes will not disrupt the balance seriously.

Feeding solid food by three weeks of age or soon after their eyes are open will start the weaning process which is planned for around six weeks. Start by moistening the puppy food. The mother can be taken away several hours before so that the puppies will be hungry and mother will not be tempted to eat it herself. From three to six weeks, feed the puppies at least four times a day or free choice and slowly decrease the amount of food given to the mother. This gets the puppies eating their new food and reduces the mother's production. During this time we are taking the mother away for longer periods of time, which she probably appreciates. We are preparing for the day when the mother will not be returned and weaning is complete. On the day of weaning leave the puppies in familiar surroundings and remove the mother.

- puppy nutrition is critical to their entire life
- proper nutrition starts with the mother
- colostrum is paramount
- monitor weight gains and stools
- help mother out if necessary
- overfeeding can be more detrimental than underfeeding
- purchase high quality puppy food
- caution when supplementing
- start planning for weaning early
- stay on grower until nine months of age

LIVER TREATS

Liver, natures " miracle food " makes tasty treats for puppies.

Chicken livers	**1 lb**	**500 g**
Whole wheat flour	**1 cup**	**250 g**
Butter (melted)	**1 tbsp**	**15 mL**
Egg yolks (beaten)	**2**	**2**
Egg whites (stiffly beaten)	**2**	**2**
Garlic powder	**1/2 tsp**	**2 mL**

In medium size bowl, mix flour, melted butter and beaten egg yolks. Cover and refrigerate for 3 to 12 hours. Just before use, add stiffly beaten egg whites. Dip livers into batter and fry in deep fat heated to 365^0 F (185^0 C) until reasonably brown. Cool and give to puppies individually as treats.

When making recipes for puppies, some ingredients are better than others. Use high Biological Value animal protein ingredients. Grains and vegetables have the same considerations as for adults. Chicken and pork fat is more easily digested. Infant human vitamin preparations work well. Yogurt is better than straight cow or goat milk.

SICK PUPPY CARE

About one quarter of all puppies born alive die within the first week of life and another one tenth in the second week. Causes include being crushed by an obese mother in confined quarters, starvation, and cold. Another cause has been termed the "fading puppy" syndrome. This is a very critical time.

Be sure that the whelping box is large enough for the whole family or that there is an area where the puppies can be safe from being laid on. A bar placed across the corners, or along the sides, about three inches above the floor and three to four inches out from the wall allows some protection.

The first suck of colostrum is very important in that this milk is rich in nutrients and antibodies. If the mother is short of milk or the puppies are orphaned, refer to the section on mothers and orphan puppies (page 186 and 195).

Warm temperatures, as high as 85 - 90^0 F (30 -32^0 C) are necessary during the first week. If the puppies become chilled and cold their body functions slow down and the mother may reject them. Warming them up slowly and getting them nursing must be done.

Starvation (hypoglycemia) and dehydration happen very rapidly with the new born, so get veterinary attention quickly if the situation cannot be corrected at home. The veterinarian will administer glucose and electrolytes and also oxygen if required.

The "fading-puppy" syndrome seems to be a combination of several things. Puppies appear normal at birth but die within a few days. Cold puppies that become infected with disease organisms and develop other complications of the heart and lungs is believed to be the cause of their deaths. Good management and awareness at whelping will help prevent the problem. Veterinary assistance may be called for.

An orphan is a puppy that does not have access to the natural milk of the mother. This can be the result of the death of the mother or her inability to allow nursing. This inability could be because of surgery such as a caesarean section, mammary gland infection, (mastitis) or from uterine infection (metritis). Whatever the situation, puppies must be fed and raised as orphans.

If we are to take on this task, we must be prepared. The task is very demanding and time consuming and requires strict attention to detail and keen observation. It is not difficult but can be frustrating. Some basic guidelines will help our success.

Our goal is to have a steady weight gain from day one with normal stools. These are the best indicators of good health and diet.

Environment: all puppies need a very warm environment.

- 86^0 F (30^0 C) for the first five days of life
- gradually reduced to 80^0 F (27^0 C) for the second and third weeks
- then 75^0 F (23^0 C) for the fourth to sixth weeks
- to 70^0 F (21^0 C) by the eighth week

Additional heat can be provided either with a covered heating pad or a heat lamp. A thermometer should be hung and monitored and the puppies must be able to move away from the heat source if they desire.

The place of rearing should be clean, warm and free of drafts and noise. A box divided into compartments or individual boxes are fine. The puppies should be separated for the first two to three weeks of life. Separation allows for better monitoring of stool consistency and prevents the puppies from sucking their siblings' tails, genitals and ears etc.

If the relative humidity is low, pans of water or a humidifier should be nearby; puppies are very susceptible to dehydration.

Weight: the puppies should be weighed every day and should be gaining.
- one to two grams/day for every pound of desired adult weight
  (a forty lb adult; the pup should gain forty to eighty g
  (1.5 - 2.5 oz) per day until five months of age)
- birth weight should double in the first eight to ten days
- Most dogs by four months are half grown
- rapid growth continues until six to nine months

A gram scale works well and we should keep a record of the daily weights.

Milk: If at all possible, try to get the first milk or colostrum from the mother for the puppies. Colostrum is rich in maternal antibodies, the very important substances that will protect the puppies from infectious diseases until they are able to produce their own.

Bitch's milk is higher in protein and fat content than cow's or goat's milk. There are very good commercial preparations available today for orphans. Several recipes are included for home preparation.

Feeding: Puppies should be fed six times a day from birth to three weeks of age, then four times daily from three to six weeks of age.

The amount and frequency is really determined by the condition and weight gain of the puppies. Satisfied puppies are gaining weight, plump, quiet and spend most of their time sleeping. Pups that are restless, cry and fuss will not gain.

Method: Nipples and bottles are the best. Eye droppers make it difficult to gauge the amount, and feeding too fast, too much or into the lungs can result. Make the hole in the nipple large enough that milk will drip out when the bottle is inverted. If the hole is too large, the puppy may choke and if it is too small, the puppy may become discouraged. Always warm the milk to body temperature, and tip the bottle up so no air will be swallowed.

Puppies must be burped after each feeding. This is done by sitting the pup upright and bouncing gently while massaging the abdomen. All feeding equipment should be washed in hot soapy water and rinsed thoroughly in hot water after each use.

We must replace the licking and grooming normally done by the mother. It is especially important to gently rub the anus and genitals with a cotton ball moistened in baby oil to stimulate urination and defecation. Whimpering indicates a need to eliminate so continue the massaging. Wiping the eyes daily with baby oil until open is also a good idea.

Weaning: We can start the weaning process at three weeks by putting a shallow dish of soft gruel in with the puppies. A good quality puppy food, wet but not soupy, starts the puppies on solid food. Some breeders start this after the eyes are open as the curious pup will investigate. Gradually reduce the amount of water used as hard food is good exercise for the young jaws and teeth. We can use the milk formula to wet the solid food. All the time we are gradually decreasing the amount of bottle feedings, so that by six weeks the puppies are off milk and on to dry food. Fresh, clean water should always be available.

At three weeks when we start with the solid food we may leave it with the puppies or we can feed three or four times a day. By doing this with the water as well, we can start to paper train the pups by feeding and watering them and then allowing them to defecate and urinate in a contained area. Taking advantage of the oral-anal reflex in this way makes paper training more natural. The reflex is simply the desire to eliminate shortly after eating or drinking.

Summary

- orphans require a lot of attention
- warmth is a must
- weigh regularly to monitor gains
- keep environment clean, warm, and humid
- first milk or colostrum is essential
- milk replacer should be the same as natural milk
- develop a feeding routine and do not overfeed
- watch for diarrhea and dehydration
- correct size nipple holes and burping are essential
- massaging replaces mother's licking
- start on solid foods early
- plan for weaning and paper training after three weeks
- a ticking clock can simulate a mother's heartbeat and adds comfort to a lonely orphan

MILK REPLACEMENT RECIPES

Milk, cow or goat (3 1/2% fat)	1 cup	250 mL
Egg yolk	1 lg.	1 lg.
Infant vitamins (human)	2 drops	2 drops
Corn oil	1 tsp	5 mL
Cod liver oil	2 drops	2 drops

(refer to Appendix II page 237 to compare cow and goat milk nutrients) Mix and refrigerate. Warm to body temperature before feeding. Feed as much as the puppy will eat or when their tummies are full and they are content.

Whole cow's milk	3 1/2 cups	800 mL
Cream 12%	1 cup	250 mL
Egg yolk	1 lg.	1 lg.
Bone meal (steamed)	1 tsp.	6 g
Vitamin A	2000 IU	2000 IU
Vitamin D	500 IU	500 IU
Citric acid	1 tsp.	6 g

Mix, refrigerate and warm to body temperature. Vitamins can be obtained from your veterinarian.

Spaying a female dog or neutering a male should not increase the dog's weight. The dog's activity level may be lessened due to the removal of the reproductive organs and their subsequent hormones. However, the decrease in activity may be due to obesity and a lack of exercise. Neutered individuals have the same nutrient requirements as intact dogs with the exception of fewer calories. The same guidelines for feeding apply. Monitor the dogs condition, weigh regularly and feed accordingly.

Osteoporosis may be a concern that we can discuss with our dog's veterinarian as the dog gets older. Thinning of the bones may develop in later life in spayed females much the same as with menopausal women. Here, the best prevention is a well balanced diet throughout life including adequate calcium and phosphorus with vitamin D and regular exercise. High meat diets are low in calcium and high fiber diets tend to bind calcium, so foods high in this mineral should be included in the diet. Foods like yogurt and cheeses increase the absorption of calcium. If in doubt, talk to your veterinarian.

COMING HOME FROM SURGERY

Spaying is abdominal surgery, so a concentrated, nutritious diet given in small amounts, is appropriate.

Farina (Cream of Wheat ®) cooked to make 2 cups	**1/2 cup**	**125 mL**
Liver	**1 lb**	**500 g**
Butter	**1 tbsp.**	**15 mL**
B complex tablet (crushed)	**1**	**1**
Vitamin C tablet (crushed)	**250 mg**	**250 mg**

Cook farina according to directions. Chop the liver into cubes and lightly fry in butter. Mix into the cream of wheat with vitamins. Serve warm in four equal portions during the day to a 30 - 40 lb (14 - 18 kg) dog.

FEEDING SPORTING AND WORKING DOGS

" All great dogs, like all great men, work not because they have to, but because they want to. Action is their chief medium of happiness."
    Ralph Fleesh (1910)

" You cannot beat the winning combination of a well-managed conditioning program and a complete, balanced, meat-based diet."
    Harris Dunlap, Sled Dog Trainer

Sporting and Working dogs include dogs of breeds that have been selected and bred to perform a specific function, some breeds going back for centuries. Performing these functions required a lot of physical and mental exertion. The breeds developed from individual dogs that were especially suited to perform the duties asked of them. The many tasks included hunting, retrieving, pulling sleds, herding cattle or sheep and guarding. Performing and excelling in these areas required not only an athletically sound body and mind but also proper diet, training and conditioning. Breeding, conformation, and training are not in the scope of this book, but we shall discuss feeding as it applies to the working dogs in general, as each activity and breed is different.

First we must learn the difference between "fit and fat" as it applies to the working dog. Fit is not fat. The fit dog in peak condition will be on the "lean side"; we will be able to feel the individual ribs with a moderate layer of fat covering. The muscles of the legs and back should be firm and the stomach tucked up, not loose and flabby. The dog should not have any excess "baggage". A lean dog maximizes efficient heat elimination, and does not have to expend as much energy moving around. Extra weight also means added stress on the bones and joints. Mentally, a dog in peak condition, will be alert, behave well, respond positively and have a good appetite. The fit dog will work to his or her capabilities and recover quickly.

Feeding the working or active dog requires the same amount of awareness and commitment as feeding dogs in other stressful situations.

The dog is different from us in several respects. He has more heart and muscle in comparison to his total body weight. The forebearers of all dogs, "Canis Lupus", are carnivores that thrived on predominately animal flesh, high in protein and fat. The cardio-respiratory system, (heart and lungs) is superior to that in humans, and dogs do not sweat. Depending on the breed, the dog has better aerobic and anaerobic capacity than us. These differences become important when feeding the working dog if peak performance is to be reached and maintained.

Aerobic and anaerobic simply means with air and without air. Aerobic metabolism of energy is the long endurance type of muscular activity that uses inspired oxygen, the "second-wind" that athletes talk about. Anaerobic metabolism is the type of work the muscles do without a demand for inspired oxygen. Short, quick sprints would be an example. Scientists have identified different types of muscle fibers in dogs as being aerobic or anaerobic. The long distance endurance breeds, such as the arctic sled dogs, have more aerobic fibers. Researchers have also found that these fibers contract relatively slowly and work best with fats (lipids). The anaerobic fibers found more in the sprinting breeds, such as the greyhound, contract very rapidly, and there tends to be an accumulation of lactic acid in the muscles after exertion, contributing to soreness and stiffness.

Due to the difference in muscle fibers and type of activity sled dogs can eat up to forty percent of their dry matter diet as fat. For fast running sprinters about eight to ten percent fat is adequate, and they can receive the rest of their energy supply from carbohydrates. Fat has 2.2 times the amount of calories than carbohydrates.

The type of activity and the breed will determine the feed formulation. It is generally agreed that the working dog should get at least twenty-five percent protein in their diet. Those dogs on a high fat diet require more protein in proportion as well as magnesium. Energy levels for the average sporting dog should be about 1800 Calories/lb,(4000 C/kg) of dry matter and for sled dogs 2300, (5000) Calories.

Recommendations include adding extra minerals and vitamins. Calcium should be at two to three percent and phosphorus 1 - 1.2% and doubling the fat soluble and tripling the water soluble vitamins are also recommended. Fiber level of less than two percent is recommended and no extra salt as dogs do not sweat.

Water is always important. Cool water is more palatable and helps cool the dog off. Water should be given before work and during their activities because they lose a lot during exertion.

One person, knowledgeable in monitoring body condition, should be in charge of feeding. Every dog is different; some are "hard keepers" and others "easy keepers" with others in-between.

Amounts fed will vary with the season and activity. In the off season, a quality maintenance formulation is sufficient. Nearer to the time of training and events, the amount and formulation will change. Depending upon the level of training and work, allow enough lead time to build up the dogs and get them used to the higher density rations.

Feeding in preparation for the event is also a consideration. If the activities require short fast spurts of energy, a certain degree of "carb loading" can be done just as with the human athlete. The food eaten the night before, such as pasta, is high in simple carbohydrates, and the liver and muscles are "loaded" with glycogen in preparation for the quick bursts of energy that will be needed.

Endurance trainers might use a method called "fat adaptation" because of the aerobic type of activity and the high fat diets. The high fat diet is increased so that the dogs are carrying a little extra by race day. The day before the race or the first day of a three day event, the daily ration is reduced by twenty-five percent, on day two and day three the dogs receive the usual amount; however, the day after the race are given fifty percent more. The idea here is that the dogs are built up with body fat reserves before the race. Near race day they are asked to start utilizing these body stores of energy that will fuel them through the race. Right after, the extra is to start replenishing the body stores in preparation for the next race.

Some general guidelines depending on the activity performed.

Classification	Activity type	Ration
Retrievers Labs, Goldens	swimming, sprints	simple carbohydrates proteins
Field Pointers & Setters	long, endurance	fats, proteins
Hunting Hounds, Beagles	running, endurance	fats, proteins
Herding Collies, Heelers	running, endurance	fats, proteins
Sled Huskys	running, endurance	fats, proteins
Coursing Greyhounds	sprinting, bursts	simple carbohydrates
Guide Labs, Shepherds	slower	maintenance
Guarding Shepherds, Dobermans	demanding bursts, cool temperatures	fats, carbohydrates
Police Shepherds	steady with bursts	carbohydrates, proteins, fats

If the activity is more of an endurance type where the energy metabolism is more aerobic, feed the higher fat and protein diets. Where the activity calls for quick bursts and is anaerobic, the diet can utilize more easily digestible carbohydrate.

ENDURANCE BANQUET

Special meal for a job well done. High in protein, fat and vitamins.

Regular Ground Beef or Pork	**2 lb.**	**1 kg**
Eggs	**2**	**2**
Butter or vegetable oil	**2 tbsp.**	**30 mL**
Left-over potatoes, rice or pasta	**1/2 cup**	**125 mL**
Bonemeal	**1 tbsp.**	**15 mL**
Baking soda (sodium bicarbonate)*	**1 1/2 tsp.**	**7 mL**
Multi-vitamin tablet (crushed)	**1**	**1**
B complex tablet (crushed)	**1**	**1**
Vitamin C tablet (crushed)	**250 mg**	**250 mg**
Vitamin E capsule	**200 IU**	**200 IU**

With butter or oil in frying pan add meat and left-overs. Add eggs and other ingredients. Can crush the egg shells as well and add. Mix well and heat to body temperature. Serve warm. Feeds a 50 - 70 lb (23 -32kg) dog one meal.

SPRINTER POWER

High in easily digested carbohydrates. Good the night before a work-out.

Cooked noodles	**1 cup**	**250 mL**
Cottage cheese	**1 cup**	**250 mL**
Butter or vegetable oil	**1 tbsp.**	**15 mL**
Bonemeal	**1 tbsp.**	**15 mL**
Baking Soda (sodium bicarbonate)*	**1 1/2 tsp.**	**7 mL**
Multi-vitamin (crushed)	**1**	**1**
B complex tablet (crushed)	**1**	**1**
Vitamin E capsule	**200 IU**	**200 IU**
Garlic powder	**1 tbsp.**	**15 mL**

Prepare noodles according to package directions. Drain add oil or butter and cheese. Mix in other ingredients well. Serve warm. Feeds a 50 - 70lb (23 -32kg) dog one meal.

* Baking soda (alkaline) is in the recipe to help prevent muscle damage and soreness due to lactic acid build up during exertion.

*"The problem with nothing to do, is that you can't stop
for a rest."*
        author unknown

Growing old is unavoidable and with age certain changes
occur within the dog's body. Dogs age faster than we do, but
with good nutrition throughout their lives, this process need
not be dramatic. Comparing ages for example: a dog at 1 year
= 15 years in people, 2 = 24, 3 = 28, 6 = 40, 9 = 52 and 12 =
64. Large breeds of dogs reach maturity more slowly however
their life span is shorter. A dog of the giant breed at one year
would be to twelve years for us but considered old at five.
Other dogs mature faster and live longer.

Not all dogs age at the same rate, each will vary depending on
breed, environment, diet, general health and activity level
through out their lives. As dogs age, decreases occur with the
possibility of certain problems arising.

Decreased	**Potential Problems**
sensitivity to thirst	dehydration
temperature regulation	less tolerant to cold or heat
sense of smell and taste	loss of appetite and weight
immune response	greater susceptibility to illness
restful sleep	irritability
activity and metabolism	obesity
tooth and gum health	reduced food intake
digestive function	constipation and flatulence
skin elasticity	susceptibility to skin disease
kidney function	nutrient deficiencies
hormone production	diabetes, cysts and tumors
cardio vascular function	heart, blood and vessel
lung function	bronchitis and emphysema
muscle and bone mass	loss of tone and bone fractures

All of these changes and more are inevitable. Being aware of
these changes, we can help to slow down the process and
maintain our pets' health and well-being in their later years.
As dogs age, they become quite sensitive to deficiencies or
excesses of nutrients.

We can respond to the changes. Warming and moistening the food may help appetite and water intake. Regular check- ups should be part of an old dog's itinerary. Overfeeding and obesity are the first steps in shortening the life span of our dog. As he slows down in his daily activity, we must reduce the number of calories that we feed. Reasonable physical activity maintains muscle tone, promotes circulation, improves elimination and reduces the threat of obesity.

Protein must be of good quality for the older dog so that there is adequate digestion, absorption and utilization of all the amino acids. Animal protein sources tend to be best. Excesses, however, can be a problem for the liver and kidney. Fat quality, as with protein, is essential. The fatty acids are important, especially for a healthy skin. Poultry and pork fat are better than beef tallow.

Carbohydrates have the same effects on the aged dog. Raw carbohydrates are poorly digested and must be properly cooked. Soy flour has been shown to be unusable. Fiber levels and quality are critical in the older dog. Peanut, rice and soy hulls are poor quality, whereas beet pulp, tomato or apple pomace are considered better. High fiber diets may be ineffective and harmful to older dogs; reduce the calories instead.

Greater vitamin amounts are required in the older dog, particularly vitamins A, B complex, C and E. Even though the dog can make his own vitamin C, supplementation has been beneficial, especially for gum and mouth health. Again a balanced diet is the top priority and excess supplementation a precaution, as the older dog may not be as able to tolerate the excess as a younger dog might. Zinc uptake has been found to decrease with age just as with low protein and high fiber diets. Poor hair growth and skin problems may be corrected with Zinc. Ask advice from your veterinarian as to amounts of Zinc. Older dogs should not get excess amounts of phosphorus or sodium. Excess sodium (salt) promotes retention of fluids, hypertension, cardiovascular and kidney problems.

A simple senior's recipe prepared from ingredients on hand.

Cooked rice, or pasta	**2 cups**	**500 mL**
Egg	1	1
Cottage Cheese	**1/2 cup**	**125 mL**
Vegetable Oil	**2 tbsp.**	**30 mL**
Kelp	**1 tbsp.**	**15 mL**
Brewer's Yeast	**2 tbsp.**	**30 mL**
Bone Meal	**1 tbsp.**	**15 mL**
Garlic Powder	**1 tbsp**	**15 mL**

Mix ingredients and warm in microwave. Will feed a 30 - 40 lb (14 - 18kg) dog one day.

The vitamin mineral supplements on page 150 & 151 can be used.

PENSIONER'S BIRTHDAY PARTY CASSEROLE

A gourmet meal fit for a King or Queen.

Cooked Turkey or Chicken	**1 cup**	**250 mL**
Bacon Fat or Vegetable oil	**2 tbsp.**	**30 mL**
Lasagne noodles	**8**	**8**
Egg	**1**	**1**
Wheat germ oil	**1 tbsp.**	**15 mL**
Bone meal	**1 tsp.**	**5 mL**
Garlic powder	**1/4 tsp.**	**1 mL**

Cook noodles as directed on the package. Drain. Line bottom of 8 X 8 inch (20 x 20 cm) pan. In medium sized bowl, mix chopped turkey or chicken with bacon fat, egg, wheat germ oil and bone meal. Spoon over noodles and spread. Cover with layer of noodles and sprinkle with garlic powder. Bake 30 minutes in 350⁰ F (180⁰ C) oven. Let stand for 15 minutes before cutting. Will serve a 30 - 40 lb (14 - 18kg) dog 2 days.

HANNIBAL'S HAMBURGER HASH

A tasty hamburger and ground vegetable meal.

Ground Beef	**1 lb.**	**500 g**
Peas, frozen or fresh	**1/2 cup**	**125 mL**
Carrots, sliced	**1/2 cup**	**125 mL**
Butter	**1 tbsp.**	**15 mL**
Water	**1/2 cup**	**125 mL**

Blend peas, carrots and water in blender. Brown ground beef with butter in frying pan. Mix in mashed vegetables and a 1/4 cup of Geriatric Vitamin Mix (see below). Cool and serve. Serves a 30 - 40 lb (14 - 18kg) dog one day

Peas and carrots can be substituted with vegetable and fruit trimmings.

GERIATRIC VITAMIN MIX

Adapted, with permission, from Joan Harper's The Healthy Cat and Dog Cookbook.

Bran	**1 cup**	**250 mL**
Wheat germ	**1 cup**	**250 mL**
(keep out unless refrigerating the complete mix)		
Brewers yeast	**1 cup**	**250 mL**
Lecithin	**1/2 cup**	**125 mL**
Bone meal	**1/2 cup**	**125 mL**
Kelp	**1/3 cup**	**75 mL**
Alfalfa	**1/3 cup**	**75 mL**
Magnesium oxide	**4 tsp.**	**20 mL**

Mix together and store in at least a 5 cup container. Add 1/4 cup for an average size dog's dinner. Ingredients can be obtained from the local Health Food Store.

Part Five Nutritionally Related Problems

"I have seen no end of dogs in varying states of unwellness and discomfort and traced the problem directly to nutrition."
    Wendell O. Belfield, DVM, *How To Have A Healthier Dog*

"St. Thomas, the great doctor and theologian, warns about the proper use of animals, lest they appear at the final Judgement against us: and God himself will take vengeance on all who misuse his creatures..."
    Rt. Rev. Msgr. LeRoy McWilliams

Certain conditions and diseases of the dog have a specific food related origin. Some may require the elimination of a particular food or group of foods, while others may need the addition of a supplement. Disease prevention and diagnosis by a veterinarian go hand and hand with our pet's diet. Treatment of these conditions involves some dietary management, and this is the part we will cover, things we can do at home.

I believe the two most prevalent health problems seen in our pet population today are obesity and skin conditions. I also believe that the majority of these are related to diet, either feeding too much or not enough of the required nutrients. However, it may not be that simple. If we look at diet in combination with lack of exercise, exposure to chemical pollutants, a host of medications and an ever-changing environment, we can see that the diagnosis and treatment of these conditions is complex. Everything must be considered.

To understand and treat health problems, we have to start with the "Big Picture" and examine all aspects. Our primary focus is on the digestive system from one end to the other. Some other conditions that have a relationship with diet are also discussed. We will offer first an explanation of the condition, then a discussion of dietary management.

All of these conditions or problems have many factors involved that may complicate the diagnosis, but let us try to understand the situation and how we can correct and prevent the problems for the general well-being of our dog.

A list of the main topics that will be covered in this section.

- Appetite
- Digestive System Problems
    - Mouth and Dental problems
    - Halitosis, Bad Breath
    - Stomach Problems
    - Liver
    - Pancreas
    - Intestines
    - Vomiting
    - Diarrhea
    - Constipation
    - Flatulence
    - Anal Glands
- Food Allergy and Intolerance
- Behavior Problems
- Skin Conditions
- Skeletal, Bone problems
- Bladder and Kidneys
- Heart Problems

We hope not too many factors were overlooked by simplification. With this type of an overview, we can start to appreciate how foods play a very important role in the health of our dog. Proper nutrition is an all encompassing term that can mean many things. By understanding what problems can arise from improper nutrition, we can be on our way to feeding our dog to keep him or her in a state of good health and well-being.

Nutritional management of diseases involves the treatment and prevention of deficiencies using nutrients, either to diagnose, treat, or to prevent a problem.

The desire to eat and drink is obviously an important part of nutrition and health. This desire, or appetite to eat, is basic to life. If the dog does not want to eat, something must be wrong. What does appetite do, what can change it and how can we get it back?

Appetite influences the anticipation of food as well as how much and how fast the dog will eat. The anticipation (feeding at regular times) also starts the digestive juices or enzymes flowing in preparation for food.

Factors that can modify appetite:

- full, the dog has eaten
- fasting or food deprivation
- anticipation of being fed
- smell and taste
- past experiences with a particular food
- general health
- general nutritional state
- a plugged nose
- sore mouth, teeth, gums and/or throat
- upset stomach
- pain from injury or surgery
- medications
- anxiety and depression

All of these by themselves or in combination can alter the dog's appetite. If our dog does not want to eat, we become concerned and if it should continue the cause maybe serious.

To remedy the loss of appetite, start with determining the cause and correcting it. The neighbours or someone else in the house feeding the dog might be the problem. A change in food or a dislike for the new diet could be why the dog is not eating. We can stimulate appetite often by just warming the food so that some aroma is given off. Tasty ingredients like liver, chicken, meat drippings and garlic will create some interest.

DIGESTIVE SYSTEM PROBLEMS

Mouth and Dental Problems

The mouth, teeth, tongue and throat can be affected by nutritional factors. Pain or disease in this area will also affect appetite and prevent the dog from eating and getting all nutrients.

A sore mouth and gums could be the result of a deficiency of riboflavin B_2 and the other B vitamins. A sore throat may be from "kennel cough" or tonsillitis which can decrease appetite. The most common mouth conditions, however, have to do with the teeth and gums.

Dental problems in our modern dog today stem from breeding and diet. We have selected some breeds of dogs with short jaws, bulldogs, Pekinese and pugs, for example, where the teeth may be crowded. Some toy breeds are also more prone to overlapping and retention of "baby teeth" that can lead to gum disease and sore mouths. Having this looked after can make a difference to the dog's eating habits and nutritional state. I believe that our modern dog's diet is also to blame. Soft, easy to chew foods, containing a lot of carbohydrate are a long way from the historical situation of wild dogs who chewed on bones, gristle and ate a high protein, high fat diet.

A common problem is periodontal disease. In this disease, material such as food, bacteria, and mineral deposits build up around the teeth causing the gums to recede. Inflammation and pockets develop, making matters worse. Bacterial growth can continue, not only affecting the dog's mouth, but the infection may spread to other parts of his body. Bad breath, bleeding gums, lose teeth, painful chewing, excessive salivation, lack of appetite and weight loss all can result.

Sound nutrition, including giving vitamins and minerals, help, to prevent these problems. Chewable things, such as uncooked bones, or raw hide offer the dog some exercise for the teeth and gums. Vitamins A, C, D, and B complex, as well as the minerals calcium, phosphorus and zinc, will improve these situations. Brushing and/or cleaning dogs' teeth seems to be in vogue now, but we must not forget to deal with the causes.

Halitosis, bad breath

Foul breath can be a problem, especially in older dogs, and is a sign of poor health that should be looked into. Common causes

- just eating something smelly
- tooth and gum disease
- mouth, throat or lung infection
- food allergy or intolerance
- low stomach acid with an increase in bacterial activity
- underlying illness such as diabetes or kidney disease
- certain medications and foods

Have the dog looked at by our veterinarian to determine the cause and start appropriate treatment. Again, good nutrition with all required nutrients including the vitamins and minerals, can help to prevent halitosis.

Stomach Problems

The stomach is the first stop for the swallowed food. Several problems can arise at this point. The problems can range from mild indigestion to more severe infection or cancerous growths.

Possible causes of stomach problems

- eating too fast
- swallowing a lot of air
- strenuous exercise before or after eating
- food intolerance or food allergy
- swallowing non food items like plastic, rubber or cloth
- drinking or eating chemical poisons
- continuous use of some medications
- stress
- too much or not enough production of stomach acid
- rotation or twisting of the stomach (torsion)
- infection and disease
- cancerous growths

All of these and more can, by themselves or in combination, give our dog problems. We may be able to correct the simpler problems. The more difficult we can refer to our veterinarian.

What signs will we see?

- the dog is in pain and discomfort after eating
- the abdomen may be swollen and hard: bloated
- reluctance to move and may stand with hind legs under and with an arch to his back
- may appear to "pray" with front legs kneeling and back legs standing
- usually vomits and may continue to retch
- is excessively thirsty and may drink a lot
- dog has no appetite

Stomach problems usually show more dramatic signs than those further down the digestive system such as the intestines or liver. If we suspect our dog has a stomach problem, our first step is to remove any food that may be left and watch for all the signs. We might want to save any vomited material for later analysis, and we should think back to anything that was done or fed differently. This history will all help to make a diagnosis.

Gastric Torsion or the rotation of the stomach is an emergency situation. If our dog is one of the large "barrel chested" type such as German Shepherds, Labs, Bassets or Boxer and is showing discomfort and fullness after eating, with unproductive attempts to vomit, a twist of the stomach is something to consider.

A sudden irritation to the stomach of the dog will make the dog vomit. This is his natural response. The other is to not eat anything after. Fasting, therefore, allows time for the stomach and other parts of the digestive system to heal and to avoid any more irritation. An otherwise healthy dog in good condition can go without food for several days. During this time water must always be available.

Regular feeding habits and proper nutrition are the first steps in preventing stomach problems from arising. If our dog tends to eat fast and swallow a lot of air, smaller portions given throughout the day in a private area without disturbances will help. Allow at least two hours before and after eating for exercise and keep garbage in covered containers. Play things, balls, toys etc. should be large and durable enough that they cannot be swallowed. Watch puppies to ensure that pieces of cloth or plastic are not swallowed.

A typical home treatment for a minor stomach or food related problem could be as follows

- Fast from solid foods for several days feeding only water and broths. A vitamin mineral supplement should be fed during this time, as they are required for healing.
- Next, feed bland foods that are easy to digest such as cottage cheese, cooked eggs, liver and cooked porridge.
- Gradually introduce meat and vegetable meals.
- If we thought that the original problem was the brand of commercial dog food that we were using and we want to go back to this type of diet, pick a different brand and start with a little at a time so the dog can get used to it.

Refer to Part Two Commercially Prepared Dog Food for guidance. If we suspect a food allergy or intolerance, this is covered later on page 224.

FASTING BROTH

A broth for a sensitve stomach while we are fasting the dog. (Avoid fat, milk, sugars, processed and spicy foods)

Warm water	**3 cups**	**750 mL**
Beef or chicken boullion cube	**1**	**1**
Human Infant Mult-vitamin drops	**5 drops**	**5 drops**
Vitamin C, sodium ascorbate powder	**1/2 tsp.**	**2 mL**
B complex 50 mg tablet crushed	**1**	**1**
Garlic powder	**1/4 tsp.**	**1 mL**

Dissolve the cube in the warm water then cool and add the other ingredients. Let the dog drink as much as he wants.

Liver Problems

The liver, as we stated in Part One, is the largest and one of the most important organs in the dog's body. It is responsible for taking most of the absorbed nutrients and converting and storing these nutrients for the many needs of the cells. The liver also detoxifies poisons that may be ingested. Because of these many functions, any disorders are serious to the health of the dog. Hepatitis or inflammation of the liver is the usual disorder that can be caused by a viral infection or ingestion of poisonous substances.

Symptoms of liver problems include

- nausea and vomiting
- loss of appetite
- jaundice, a yellowing of the skin, due to a back up of bile, that can be seen in the "whites" of the eyes
- pale, tan coloured stool
- an enlargement of the abdomen due to a swollen liver

Liver disease not only affects the digestion, absorption and utilization of nutrients, but the vomiting and loss of appetite also reduces the intake of important nutrients. Fasting, with the introduction of foods that will not stress the liver, is the treatment. All fats and oils should be avoided; however, the fat soluble vitamins A, D, E and K may have to be given by injection. Give vitamin A instead of beta carotene as the liver may have difficulty in converting beta carotene to vitamin A.

Feeding easily digested high quality proteins, carbohydrates, vitamins and minerals is required to provide adequate nutrition for healing and repair of the damaged tissues at the same time trying not to stress the liver any more than necessary.

Small portions fed four to five times a day should be the routine. Be prepared to follow this for a month or more as the healing process takes a long time.

Pancreatitis, inflammation of the pancreas, is a serious problem for the dog. A condition that also involves the pancreas is diabetes, or a lack of sufficient insulin production. Dietary management for the two are the same. With diabetes, insulin injections may have to be given. The pancreas is involved with digestion and utilization of nutrients as well as the production of insulin. From blood and urine, a diagnosis can be made.

The prime suspects are older, overweight dogs that have a long history of poor nutrition and eating a lot of sweet and fat foods. These are often dogs with advancing age that are getting little exercise and extra love in the form of sweet and fat foods. The pancreas just becomes overloaded. Watch dog foods with a lot of sugar in them.

Once the pancreas cannot function, the dog will stop eating, vomit often, have diarrhea, be weak and may cry in pain. Have the veterinarian look at the dog and if the pancreas is the problem, start the diet and life style change.

Refer to the Section on overweight dogs on page 177 and start a regular exercise program. As well as reducing the number of calories fed, avoid fats and oils, including cod liver oil, as these can irritate the pancreas as it heals. Use capsules for the fat soluble vitamins, A, D, & E, or get an injection for the dog from the veterinarian which will last up to two months. Give vitamin C (sodium ascorbate 1/4 tsp. 1/2 tsp. per day depending on the size of the dog) as well as the water soluble B vitamins.

Fruits and vegetables will be especially hard for the dog to digest, so wait until he is better to give these foods. As in liver disease give bland, easy to digest, high quality animal proteins. Zinc and vitamin D have lately been suggested to be important for the pancreas in its production of insulin. As we said earlier, the pancreas not only produces digestive enzymes, but it also manufactures insulin for the utilization of blood sugars for energy.

Pancreatic problems require a combined effort of treatment and prevention that involve our veterinarian, diet, and exercise.

Vomiting

Vomiting is something that dogs can do very easily. This ability to evacuate the stomach is a trait that they have acquired from their wild ancestors. As we stated in Part One, vomiting is an asset. If, in their hurry, they eat harmful fragments of sharp bones or irritating chemical substances, throwing up is a way to get rid of it.

Should our dog occasionally throw up his meal, we do not have to become too concerned. However, if this continues with repeated retchings, professional help must be sought. This is also true if our dog vomits after every meal and appears unable to keep anything down.

Causes for vomiting that arouse our concern

  • bacterial or viral infection
  • foreign body obstructions
  • poisoning
  • stomach problems
  • drug medications
  • gall bladder problems
  • liver problems
  • pancreas problems
  • kidney problems
  • intestinal problems
  • pain such as after surgery
  • excitement and/or stress

Because vomiting is just a sign or symptom of something else, we have to get to the root cause and correct it. Once this has been determined, then the treatment can be started. Nutrition plays a part in the recovery but can be difficult if nothing can be kept down. Dehydration and electolyte (minerals such as sodium and potassium) loss may be to such an extent that intravenous feeding may be necessary. Withholding all food and water and giving the dog ice cubes or the popsicles (page 173) can help. Try bland foods, as discussed for stomach problems, once the dog appears to be able to hold something down. Vitamins may have to be given by injection at this time.

Diarrhea, the opposite of constipation, is characterized by soft, unformed stools. The dog's digestive system is responding to some irritation or disorder. Pushing the contents of the intestines through quickly is the defense mechanism to get rid of the irritant. Because the speed of passage is rapid there is little absorption of water by the large intestine so the stools are not formed and the material is quite liquid. Diarrhea can occur from a simple change in diet or a food sensitivity. Lack of one or more digestive enzymes can produce diarrhea as well as excitement or anxiety. If this continues for some time, the consequences can be serious. Dehydration and loss of vital minerals, called electrolytes, can be life threatening. This is especially true for young puppies. Several hours of diarrhea for a puppy may be long enough to be fatal.

Possible irritants include viruses, bacteria, chemicals, worms, spoiled foods, foreign bodies, and antibiotics. Foods such as milk, ice cream, vegetables and fruits can also cause diarrhea. As we have said before, dogs do not have the lactase enzyme for lactose; the milk sugar and their short intestine is unsuited for ideal plant or vegetable digestion.

Seek a reason for the diarrhea and eliminate the cause, rather than treating the symptom. Obtaining a diagnosis will include a history of what the dog has eaten in the last twelve hours and what he or she was in contact with as well as activities or sources of stress. Remember, diarrhea is a natural occurrence for flushing out the digestive system and to stop the diarrhea may be working against this safety mechanism.

A simple approach to treatment is to fast the dog of all solid food for at least forty-eight hours. (Nature does this anyway when the dog loses its appetite) Fasting allows the intestine to rest. Water must not be restricted. Easily digested, bland foods, such as soups and broths, give some nourishment at this time as well as fluids and electrolytes.

Diarrhea is the mechanism by which the dog is attempting to get rid of an undesirable substance. It is up to us to allow the process to work. If this should continue so that the loss of fluids and other nutrients have gone too far, then we must intervene. Veterinary treatment at this stage is essential.

Identifying what is causing the diarrhea is our first concern. The loss of appetite, or self induced fast, is the dog's own means of attacking the problem, giving the digestive system a rest and allowing time to heal.

Some old time remedies and holistic type treatments would include giving mineral oil at the first signs of diarrhea. This was to help the dog's body to flush out the irritating substances and offer some protection to the inner walls of the intestine. Producing a diarrhea with this treatment perhaps prevented some damage before it became extensive. Other treatments are kaopectate and activated charcoal. These substances, while absorbing the offending substances, also firm up the stools and reduce the fluid and electrolyte loss. Long term use of these treatments is not advisable in that the digestive process and nutrient absorption can be hindered.

WARM FORTIFIED BROTH

A tasty broth that will not aggravate the intestine but gives water and nutrients that may be lost.

Chicken or Beef bullion cube	1	1
(Chicken or		
Beef Broth soup 1 can)		
Water	3 cups	750 mL
Baking Soda ®	1/2 tsp.	2 mL
Garlic powder	1/4 tsp.	1 mL

Dissolve the cube in hot water, or prepare the soup as directed on the can or package. Cool, mix in the baking soda (to replace the bicarbonate lost), garlic powder and serve.

These guidelines are for the adult dog. Puppies require veterinary attention quickly, as they are very vulnerable to dehydration and complications.

At the first signs of diarrhea
- get outside or somewhere the dog can defecate freely
- carefully clean up after the dog
- remember some infections called zoonoses can infect us and our family
- fresh clean drinking water is always available
- start the detective work to find the cause
  - was there a change in diet?
  - did the dog get into something that he shouldn't have?
  - is this more than a food problem, is fever present?
  - when was the dog last tested for worms?
  - did we start medication recently?
  - was there a recent cause for excitement or stress?
- remove food (place in air tight container and keep cool; we may want to have it tested for toxins or bacteria)
- fast from solid foods for twenty-four to forty-eight hours
- if our dog wants to eat start with the soups and broth
- use easily digested quality foods next
- if regular food was not the problem, gradually start back
- reduce the regular proportions and feed more often

Ingredients to use: lean ground meats, liver, cottage cheese, yogurt, eggs and consomme.
Ingredients to avoid: fats, oils, milk, ice cream, breads, cereals and flour, vegetables and fruits.

Because the dog is a carnivore we give animal protein source foods and stay away from hard to digest plant or vegetable products until his digestive system has settled down.

Can try: Mom's Chicken Soup   on page 184.
           Hospital Porridge   on page 184.

Constipation

Constipation usually means difficulty in passing stools, reluctance to pass stools or hard dry stools. There are many causes for these signs, so a diagnosis is essential in that the constipation may not be dietary. Some common non dietary causes could be an obstructed bowel, bowel infection, illness with fever, dehydration, stress, drug therapy, old age, lack of exercise or impacted anal glands. Dietary causes may include poor quality dog food, lack of water, food sensitivity and low fiber diets. There are other things that will look like constipation, so have a veterinarian examine the dog.

Things that we can do for constipation concerning the diet

- increase the fiber intake, foods like whole grains, vegetables, fruits and seeds.
- avoid poor quality dog foods
- eliminate fatty refined foods, sugar and salt
- provide regular exercise
- supply good quality water
- try raw meat
- sprinkle 1/2 - 1 tsp. of bran on the food once a day
- add cooking oil: 1 tsp. to 1 tbsp. to the food
- add 250 - 500 mg of vitamin C to diet per day

HIGH FIBER - LAXATIVE

Try this raw meat high fiber recipe if the dog has the need for a simple laxative meal.

Ground beef	**1 lb**	**500 g**
All Bran ®		
(or Bran Flakes ®)	**1 cup**	**250 mL**
Vegetable oil	**2 tbsp.**	**30 mL**
Garlic powder	**1/4 tsp.**	**1 mL**
Vitamin C	**500 mg**	**500 mg**

Mix all the ingredients, warm to body temperature and serve. Will feed a 25 lb (11 kg) dog one day.

Flatulence is the medical term for the excessive production of gas. This gas is then passed either anally or orally. The production of some gas in the digestive tract is normal; however, when it becomes excessive and foul, we become concerned.

Excessive flatulence can result from the type of food eaten or from a malfunction in the digestive system.

Gas production is primarily the result of bacterial fermentation of the various foods eaten. Herbivores tend to have a lot of gases formed in their digestive systems in that they must rely on bacterial activity for digestion of the plant material that they eat. When we feed our dog more vegetable type foods, especially beans, cabbage, and onions, for example, the gas formed may be offensive.

Increased fermentation can occur if there is an overgrowth of bacteria in the digestive tract due to a slowdown in the passage of food through the system. Any of the problems of the stomach, pancreas or intestines, including worms, decreases the ability for the digestive system to work. The food stays in the system longer allowing the fermentation to occur.

Food intolerances, constipation, stomach, liver, pancreas, and intestinal problems can all lead to excessive gas production. Again, if our dog should have a lot of foul gas, we should try to find the root cause as flatulence is a symptom of something else.

If we are feeding our dog a low quality dog food containing a lot of vegetable material or we are feeding a lot of the same, be prepared for gas. Try experimenting with different foods to see if the culprit food can be identified. Animal proteins and fats are digested quickly by the carnivore, so they should not produce much flatulence; however, if these foods do, perhaps the problem is not the kind of food but rather a problem with the dog's digestive system.

FOOD INTOLERANCES AND ALLERGIES

First, let's look at the difference between a food allergy and a food intolerance. An allergy is a response by the dog's immune system to an antigen, or foreign substance. When the dog came in contact with the antigen earlier, antibodies were made to counteract what the dog's body considered undesirable. If the dog comes in contact with this substance later an immune reaction occurs. These reactions can vary from runny nose and eyes to reddening and itching of the skin as the dog's body attempts to remove or "wall-off" this undesirable substance.

A food intolerance is basically the inability to digest or utilize a particular food, so it is passed out without the dog receiving any benefit.

Itching, with or without diarrhea, may indicate a food allergy. It is my opinion that food allergies are not as common in the dog as compared to food intolerances.

A food intolerance typically is seen as just diarrhea as the dog's digestive system cannot "tolerate" a particular food. Diarrhea may result from eating too much or too fast, or a change in diet and not necessarily a specific food problem. Often the digestive system and bowel will just need some time to get used to the different diet. When changing dog foods or trying a new recipe, especially those with a lot of vegetables or fruits, start out with small portions then increase over several days to avoid too big a change.

Milk and milk products such as ice cream given to an adult dog often results in diarrhea. This we could call an intolerance in that the dog, as we said earlier, does not have the enzymes to digest the milk sugar lactose. Therefore, the undigested milk portions are flushed (diarrhea) out of the system.

With the help of our dog's veterinarian, a record of all foods eaten and any changes in the environment (a new house plant) will help in the diagnosis. Once suspected, eliminating the culprit foods that cause these reactions can confirm the diagnosis.

Clearly the ideal solution is to eliminate and avoid the offending food. The difficulty is in identify which one. With the great array of commercially processed dog foods on the market today, containing many ingredients from various sources, finding the exact culprit might be impossible. The dog may be reacting not only to a food ingredient but to the hundreds of chemicals and foreign substances that may be present. These include everything from additives, pesticides, herbicides to colour and artificial flavours. The list could be endless.

The usual approach is to fast the dog of all foods for several days to a week. Do not eliminate water. Then introduce specific fresh foods with close observation so that the offending food maybe be identified. Try a different brand of dog food, of which we have made note of the ingredients from the label, so that the detective process may start to identify the food. In my experience, a vitamin-mineral supplement works well here.

Lately we have seen an increase of lamb and rice preparations in commercial dog foods. The industry is responding to the demand for low allergenic type foods. It is my opinion that before we jump to too many diet changes and treatments for food allergies and skin problems, we get back to the basics. First try to get the "big picture" with regards to the complete home environment. Is the present diet deficient in any of the required nutrients especially vitamins and minerals? What is the quality of the present diet ingredients and what about sources, additives, preservatives or contaminations in storage. Using fresh home processed ingredients with attention given to the vitamins and minerals might be the final solution. Refer to Skin Conditions on page 228 for more information.

BEHAVIOR PROBLEMS

Behavior is the way a dog acts, all the time, or in certain situations. Behavior problems are abnormal actions for that particular individual. Abnormal behavior may be related to feeding and diet; other causes might be breeding, individual personality, loneliness, fear, stress, or lack of exercise. Often more than one factor is involved.

I believe many of our dogs suffer from monotony and boredom. The ancestral wild dogs did not have time to be bored. They were constantly active either in their search for food, or mating and family raising. Time was not a commodity that they had a lot of. Contrast our modern dog who's greatest commodity is time. Food, water and a warm secure home is not a problem. If we consider this and provide activity, both physical and mental, perhaps we can limit the boredom.

Our dogs want stability in their lives. If their routines are disrupted they become upset. Scheduling regular times for feeding, exercise and play helps to insure stability.

Typical behavior changes related to diet would be those associated with skin and intestinal changes. An itchy skin with diarrhea may be the first indication of a food sensitivity. The itching and scratching can become self-mutilating and cause severe damage.

Ingredients of some commercial dog foods tend to use less animal source ingredients and more plant source starches and sugars. To maintain palatability and flavor, additives as well as preservatives are added. These additional ingredients might explain some of our dog's behavior problems.

I have found that I get a headache if I eat foods containing sugar substitutes or if I forget to wash fruit before I eat it. Dogs might react the same way. Dogs cannot talk, so a painful tooth, a headache or perhaps pain from a stomach ulcer may be bothersome enough to alter their normal happy behavior. A good medical examination may be called for.

We would all agree that coprophagy, stool eating, is a disgusting occurrence. However, we normally see it in young foals and calves. The belief is that the young are picking up bacteria or "starter" from mother's manure for their own digestive system. These good bacteria will help populate their system so that they can start digesting plant material. Is the puppy doing the same thing? I do not know; I would suspect not; the puppy and adult dog rely less on bacteria and other microorganisms to digest their foods than the vegetarian herbivores. Rather I think this behavior, which may become a habit, is probably due to a dietary deficiency or boredom. The solution is to remove the feces, maintain a clean kennel, be sure that the diet is adequate and try to eliminate the boredom.

Behavior problems are a large and encompassing topic which can involve may things including our own expectations.

From the nutritional aspect we should strive for a balanced diet with all known nutrients present. Supplements we may try include

- a vitamin/mineral supplement
- a vitamin/mineral home recipe supplement
- B complex vitamins and foods
    - B complex tablet/day (with no vitamin A or D)
    - foods: liver, kidney, eggs, beans, wholewheat
- vitamin C: 250 - 1500 mg / day
    - foods: fresh fruits (especially: papaya, & cantaloupe), peppers, broccoli, and beef liver

If feeding a commercial dog food, perhaps a change to a different brand might help. A complete home prepared diet with fresh ingredients and supplemental vitamins and minerals may have to be tried if we think that the cause may be due to additives present in the other. It may take some time to find the problem and to correct it, so keep looking and be patient.

SKIN CONDITIONS

The skin is not only the dog's largest organ, it also has the most problems. This soft flexible organ covered with hair serves the dog with protection from the elements, sensation, heat regulation, secretion and elimination. Because of the size of the skin and its complex nature, many things can go wrong. It has been said that ninety percent of skin problems originate from the inside and ten percent from the outside. Inside would include such things as improper nutrition, food allergies, hormonal problems, inheritance and disease in other body organs. Outside factors would include parasites, bacteria, chemicals and physical trauma. Skin problems occupy a large part of a veterinarian's small animal practice. I believe that skin problems and obesity are the two main medical concerns in our modern dog population today, and both are strongly associated with nutrition.

Skin problems associated with nutrition can start with the puppy before birth. If the mother has not been feed properly during her gestation the litter may have more reddened skin than normal combined with dry hair. Adequate nutrition is important for skin health even before birth.

Nutritional considerations for skin health is an ongoing process as the skin and hair are always growing and at a rapid rate. This large organ in which the cells are replaced in about three weeks requires a lot of nourishment. Poor or bad nutrition will show up almost immediately in this large, fast-growing organ, giving us a good indicator of the dog's health.

Dog's hair grows in cycles and is shed periodically, as opposed to humans' hair which is continuous. There are three phases to the cycle. During the growth phase, hair follicles are actively producing hair, pushing out the old in what we see as shedding. Then there is a resting phase when the follicles slow down. The third phase is between these two called the transitional period. The cycle is regulated by hormones depending on the environment and time of year. This determines when the dog will shed.

To specifically look at the nutrients involved, we have to start with the basics: protein, fat, vitamins and minerals. Hair is ninety-five percent protein and normal hair growth is about one hundred feet per day. Normal growth of the skin uses up about twenty-five percent or 1/4 of the daily protein requirement of the dog. Adequate, high quality protein obviously is the number one consideration in skin health. Poor quality dog foods or poor quality and low protein home diets will show thickened, darker skin and loss of hair colour. Hair may fall out in patches with other hair becoming thin, dry, dull and brittle. We will see this more in growing dogs because their demand for protein is higher.

Fat, or more specifically the three fatty acids, are important for skin and hair growth and health. Fatty acid deficiency causes dry, lusterless hair and fine scaling, thickened skin. Later, hair loss and itching may develop. Later, the skin becomes oily or greasy. This oily secretion, or sebum, at first slows down, then increases to excess. With these changes, bacterial infection can start as well as self-inflicted trauma from the itching and scratching. Poor quality dry dog foods, with inadequate fat or improperly processed combined with poor containers, can start a dog on a journey to fatty acid deficiency.

Of the vitamins, the fat soluble A and E, especially A, function to maintain a healthy skin. As we said near the beginning of the book, vitamin A is required for the epithelial cells of the dog's body. Insufficient or too much vitamin A, will give the dog a poor hair coat, hair loss, scaling of the skin and an increased susceptibility to bacterial infection. Vitamin E, selenium and the fatty acids work together as well for a healthy skin.

The water soluble vitamins B and C also play an important role in skin and hair health which may explain why a dog, fed only processed dog foods, responds to B and C supplementation with improved skin and hair health. The heat of processing and long storage depletes these water soluble vitamins.

All the B vitamins or the B complex are given, with riboflavin, niacin and biotin being especially important for the skin.

Vitamin C deficiency in man causes scurvy with hemorrhages throughout parts of the body tissues as well as broken "corkscrew" hair and thickening of the skin. Even though we believe the dog makes his own vitamin C, in times of stress and disease, he may require more than can be manufactured.

Of the minerals, zinc has been shown to be important for skin health in many animals and man. Some breeds of dogs have a decreased capacity to absorb zinc as well as dogs on high-calcium or high-cereal diets which tie-up or bind zinc. Growing puppies are especially vulnerable and will have reddened skin, followed by hair loss, crusting, scaling and then weeping areas around the mouth, chin, eyes and ears. Their coats will be dull and may develop thick crusts on the elbows and other joints. Over supplementation of vitamins and minerals will lead to other problems, so do not attempt to treat these conditions without professional help. Concentrate our efforts on prevention with adequate attention to feeding a well-balanced diet containing all of the essential nutrients.

Prevention of skin problems starts with adequate nutrition so that the skin is healthy and can resist any assaults put upon it. A balanced diet with all the correct and available nutrients of protein, fatty acids, vitamins A and E, and the minerals zinc and selenium gives this fast growing and dynamic organ a chance to do its job. Refer to Part One, Nutrition and Nutrients, for a review of how each of the nutrients plays its role in the dog's overall health.

In my veterinary experience dealing with skin problems in my animal patients, I look at the nutritional aspects first. Even if the problems are external such as parasites or bacteria, I believe that if the skin is to heal and resist further assaults, it must be fed properly so it can do it's job.

Supplements containing polyunsaturated fatty acids, vitamins A, Bs, C and E, and zinc.

Brewer's yeast	1 cup	250 mL
Sodium ascorbate powder	4 tbsp.	60 mL
Zinc sulfate 50 mg tablets, crushed	2	2
Garlic powder	1/2 tsp.	2 mL
Wheat germ oil	1/4 cup	50 mL
Cod Liver oil	1/4 cup	50 mL
Safflower oil	1/2 cup	125 mL

Mix the dry ingredients together and store in an air tight container in the refrigerator. Give 2 tbsp. every day. Mix the oils and store in an air tight container. Shake well and give 2 tbsp. every day with the dry supplement. Have enough for a week. Can mix both with regular daily meal.

JOAN HARPER'S VITAMIN AND MINERAL MIX

All powders are mixed together: 1/2 -1 tsp per meal for dogs.

2 cups brewers yeast
1 cup bone meal
1/4 cup magnesium oxide powder
1/4 cup alfalfa meal or powder
2 tablespoons kelp

JOAN HARPER'S TREATMENT FOR "DOGGIE ODOR"

1/2 tsp Vitamin/Mineral supplement
10 mg Zinc tablet
sprinkle liberal amount of sodium ascorbate (vitamin C)
garlic flakes
50 IU. vitamin E
1/2 tsp liquid lecithin

Joan claims this has done wonders for her old dog Jack and his long fur parka and his "doggie odor".

BLADDER PROBLEMS

Bladder problems in the dog usually involve cystitis and/or bladder stones. Cystitis is inflammation of the walls of the bladder and stones are mineral accumulations. Signs often seen will be no urination, difficulty or pain in passing urine, increased frequency of urination and discoloured urine.

Any or all of these signs are cause for concern, and a trip to the veterinarian for a diagnosis is called for. We shall limit our discussion to bladder stones.

Bladder stones, uroliths, may form in the bladder as a result of certain minerals crystallizing around a tiny piece of inner wall that has sluffed off. The amount of offending mineral content present in the diet and/or water and the general health of the dog will determine if these stones will form and become large enough to cause trouble. An alkaline or less acidic urine is also thought to be a contributing factor. Neutered males tend to have the most problems which I believe is due to the penis remaining smaller than in an intact male. Older dogs of both sexes can develop stones as well. If the stones become too large they cannot be passed and will continue to grow in the bladder or become lodged in the urethra or tube leading to the outside. Large stones have to be removed surgically.

Prevention involves having males neutered after they have reached the adult size and avoiding water and foods with high mineral (ash) contents. Some rural water supplies for drinking and crop production contain high levels of the offending minerals that can lead to these problem. Poor quality dry dog foods fed over extended lengths of time may also contribute to this problem as well as lack of sufficient good quality drinking water. Acidifing the urine also helps. Ascorbic acid or vitamin C supplementation and low ash diets are in order.

Low ash formulations will have to be fed if bladder stones are a nutritional problem.

Summary

I have attempted to explain in this section of Nutritionally Related Problems those conditions where diet is a consideration as a possible cause of the problem. By understanding, without over simplifying, we can try to avoid these conditions from developing in our dog. If we understand what is going on, we should be able to recognize a problem before it gets out of hand. Remember, many of the problems discussed may be a combination of several things, so the complete "big picture" has to be considered. Seek professional help when necessary.

Feeding our dog is one of the most important things we do as dog owners. Just as important is to watch and listen to our dog and realize what he or she is telling us. From appetite and behavior to breath and coat condition, the dog is telling or showing us that all is not right. It is up to us to read the signs and act accordingly.

If all is fine, our dog will show it. What we feed and how much goes a long way to preventing many problems. Our dogs lives in a different environment then their ancestors. Our dogs have many advantages when it comes to the supply of food and shelter. However, our modern dogs have to do their best when it comes to adapting to our modern pollutants, processed foods, additives and in their ability to pick and choose. Many of our dogs' problems seen today are not seen in their wild and ancestral cousins. We have changed their environment and their food.

Now and in the future we will have to do our best to understand our dogs and to supply them with those essentials that will allow them to live happy and healthy productive lives. Be it as a house pet or a working dog, the total responsibility is ours. This does not have to be difficult and the first place to start is with the food we give them to eat. Good luck, when it doubt do what nature would do.

GOING ON TRIPS

With a mobile society such as ours, we often take our pet with us either by car or by airplane. There are a few things we can do to prepare that will make the trip more comfortable for all.

- Visit the veterinarian well in advance of the trip and have all vaccinations and health certificates in order. We may want to pick up medication for motion sickness at this time.

- Purchase a good collar. Attach an identification tag with the pet's name, our name, address and phone number or some other address so that if the dog is lost we can be notified.

- If planning to stay in motels or campgrounds, ask about pets when making reservations.

- When a long trip is planned and we are not sure how the pet will travel, taking short trips in the neighbourhood will help train the dog and alert us to signs of motion sickness.

- A travel grate or portable kennel may be something we should look into especially if air travel is planned. Using the grate at home before we leave gives the dog some security later.

- Allow at least two hours before car travel and six hours before air travel with no food. Dogs can fast for many hours without harm.

- Take familiar food, toys or blankets as well as a container of water as unfamiliar water can be upsetting.

- Some people claim that an antistatic strap attached to their car helps avoid motion sickness. This could be something to try.

- Stop often to allow exercise and bathroom breaks. Use a leash and beware of other dogs that may be loose such as guard dogs around service stations and truck stops.

If, rather than taking our dog with us, we decide to board, a few items of note may help.

- Check out the facility before we commit. Ask other pet owners for recommendations and ask for a tour of the facilities. Look at the cleanliness and condition of kennels and runs. Note heating and/or air conditioning facilities as well as the freedom from drafts.

- Note smells, noises and condition of food and water dishes.

- Talk to the staff and observe their attitude and cleanliness. Ask about supervision as well as night and weekend routines.
  Inquire about exercise and after hours delivery and pick ups.

- Find out the kennel's rules with regards to vaccinations, health certificates and contracts required. Beware of payments in advance and added costs.

- We might ask to have the dog bathed before we take him home as our dog may pick up a " kennel smell " after a long stay.

- Make a list at home and bring with the dog:

  - an emergency telephone number
  - the food currently fed
  - name and telephone number of the dog's veterinarian
  - any special problems, medication, or diet instructions
  - any behavioral habits

- Consider the cost of the services and the distance away.

APPENDIX I

CVMA (Canadian Veterinary Medical Association) Pet Food Certification Program: 339 Booth Street, Ottawa, Ontario K1R 7K1 (613) 236-1162 see page 96 for standards

Pet Food Association of Canada, 1435 Goldthorpe Road, Mississauga, Ontario, L5G 3R2, (416) 891-2921 see page 96 A Canadian pet food manufacturer's Nutrition Assurance Program

United States regulation of pet food labeling:
Agencies involved:
  Food and Drug Administration, FDA
  U.S. Department of Agriculture, USDA
  Federal Trade Commission, FTC

American Feed Control Officials, AAFCO is made up of all state and federal officials (FDA, USDA, & FTC) responsible for regulating the production, labeling, distribution, and sale of animal food. The AAFCO with recommendations from trade associations such as the Pet Food Industry, PFI, the National Feed Ingredients Association, and the American Feed Industry Association has developed the regulations in the Uniform State Feed Bill. This bill allows monitoring of pet food labels, ingredients, additives, facilities and statements of nutritional adequacy. The bill also describes testing protocols for all animal feeds, label format and statements of guarantees.

AAFCO advises the state feed control officials. Pet food manufacturers must follow FDA regulations and can take legal action but rely upon the various state feed control officials for inspection and enforcement.

Comparison of 2% Cow's milk to Goat's milk

nutrient	1 cup 2% Cow milk	1 cup Goat milk
calories	121 cal	168 cal
protein	8.1 g	8.7 g
carbohydrate	11.7 g	11 g
total fat	4.7 g	10 g
saturated fat	2.9 g	6.5 g
mono-unsaturated	1.35 g	2.7 g
poly-unsaturated	0.17 g	0.36 g
cholesterol	18 mg	28 mg
vitamin A	466 IU	456 IU
vitamin C	2.3 mg	3.2 mg
vitamin D	100 IU	5 IU
vitamin E	0.09 mg	0 mg
thiamine	0.1 mg	0.1 mg
riboflavin	0.4 mg	0.3 mg
niacin	0.2 mg	0.7 mg
vitamin B6	0.1 mg	0.1 mg
vitamin B12	0.9 mcg	0.2 mcg
folate	12 mcg	1 mcg
sodium	122 mg	122 mg
calcium	297 mg	326 mg
magnesium	33 mg	34 mg
potassium	377 mg	499 mg
iron	0.1 mg	0.1 mg
zinc	1 mg	0.7 mg

A comparison of the nutrients. Cow's milk for sale in the stores are usually fortified for vitamins A, D, and E

Acid: A chemical substance that contains hydrogen atoms. Acids have a pH "power of the hydrogen" of less than 7.0. Examples of acids are vinegar and hydrochloric acid in the stomach.

Additive: A substance added to food to affect the characteristics of food such as to stabilize, cure, tenderize, fix color, flavor, season or give aromas without affecting the weight.

Aerobic: With oxygen, aerobic exercise is any steady continuous activity such as running or swimming.

Alkaline: A base, opposite of acid, having a pH of more than 7; example: Baking soda.

Allergy: A specific sensitivity which results from exposure to a particular antigen.

Amino Acid: A building block of protein; over 20 known amino acids are utilized in the body to make various proteins, such as muscle, skin, hair, nails.

Anaerobic: Without oxygen, short quick burst of muscular activity as opposed to continuous steady activity.

Anemia: The reduction in the number of red blood cells in the body, thus lowering the ability of the blood to carry oxygen.

Antibiotic: A substance made from a living organism which is capable of killing or inhibiting growth of another organism, especially bacteria; example: penicillin.

Anus: The posterior opening of the digestive system.

Antibody: Proteins made by the dog's immune system to fight against disease and infection.

Antigen: A substance (usually a protein) that stimulates an allergic reaction by the dog's immune system.

Antioxidant: A substance that protects other substances or tissues from oxygen fragments by reacting with the oxygen itself. An example is vitamin E preventing rancidity in fats.

Appetite: The desire to eat.

Avidin: A product in raw egg white that binds biotin and limits its absorption and use by the dog.

Bacteria: Microscopic one-celled organism found in the dog's body, food and all living matter.

Balanced diet: A diet in which all the known nutrients are present in the correct amounts.

Base: Opposite of Acid, an alkaline compound, pH greater than 7.

Beriberi: A disease caused by a deficiency of vitamin B_1, (thiamine) in man.

Beta Carotene: The water soluble form of vitamin A found in dark green, yellow and orange plants; example: carrots.

Bile: A fluid produced by the liver and stored in the gall bladder that is secreted into the small intestine to aid in the digestion of fat foods.

Calorie: A measurement of heat. One calorie of heat energy will raise the temperature of one gram of water (1 mL) from 14.5 C to 15.5 C. In nutrition the term calorie actually refers to a kilo-calorie or the amount of heat required to raise the temperature of one kilogram (1 L) of water one degree Celsius.

Collagen: Fibers that form scar tissue, tendons and ligaments.

Colostrum: The first milk secreted after whelping containing antibodies for the puppies to fight infection and disease.

Colouring Agents: (dyes) Synthetic or natural source substances that are mixed into or applied to various foods in order to retain or change the natural colour.

Coprophagy: The ingestion of the feces or stools.

Dehydration: Loss of water from the dog's body. Any loss greater than the normal amount required for the dog to function.

Diabetes: A condition where there is an excess of glucose in the dog's blood stream and an inability of the dog to utilize it due to a shortage of adequate insulin production by the pancreas.

Duct: A tube used for conducting fluid; example: bile duct.

Enriched, fortified food: Foods in which nutrients have been added because precooking, pasteurizing, refining, milling, or bleaching usually destroys all or part of some or all nutrients that were present in the raw form.

Eclampsia: A metabolic disorder in the whelping bitch at or near whelping seen as general weakness, convulsions and possible coma. Due to a disorder of calcium and vitamin D metabolism.

Electrolyte: A substance or salt that dissolves into positive or negative charged particles, conducts an electrical charge and is essential for the movement of body fluids; examples are sodium, potassium and chloride.

Ersatz: A substitute, something synthetic, artificial or an article used to replace something natural or genuine.

Energy: The ability to do work.

Enzymes: Complex organic substances produced by living cells that are involved in the digestion, assimilation and utilization of all nutrients. They are present primarily in raw foods as their effectiveness is destroyed by heat.

Farina: A floury substance usually made from durum wheat after the removal of the germ and bran. Can be used as noodles or as a breakfast cereal cooked in milk.

Fasting: Going without food or water or both for an extended period of time. Helpful in determining food intolerances.

Fiber: The indigestible residue of food. From carbohydrates cellulose, pectin, and hemicellulose are not digested in the dog. Hair and feathers would also be considered fiber.

Fixed formula: A commercial dog food formula in which the ingredients used do not change between manufacturing batches.

Flavouring agents: Substances made either by chemical synthesis or by extraction from natural sources and added to foods to enhance or modify the natural flavour or taste.

Flavour enhancers: Substances which do not have an inherent flavour but when added to various foods especially with a high protein content, intensify the natural taste, example monosodium glutamate (MSG).

Food Intolerance: Inability to digest a food may be due to a chemical idiosyncrasy, food contamination or lack of digestive enzyme; example: lactose intolerance.

Gastritis: Inflammation of the stomach.

Glucose: Sugar; blood sugar; the building blocks of starch.

Glycogen: The storage form of glucose in the dog's body. Formed and stored in the liver and muscles and is converted back to glucose when energy is needed.

Gram: A unit of weight. 28 grams = 1 ounce.

Hard Water: Water with a high concentration of calcium, magnesium or other substances.

Hepatitis: Inflammation of the liver.

Hormones: Biochemical substances produced by ductless glands that are secreted directly into body fluids and having specific and vital effects on other organs.

Humectants: Ingredients in soft-moist pet foods that take up water and do not allow bacteria to use it, preventing bacterial growth and spoilage; examples are propylene glycol and sorbitol.

Hydrogenation: The process in which hydrogen is added to the molecule of an unsaturated compound, such as vegetable oil. This process condenses the oil to solid texture, allowing storage without refrigeration. Most vitamins and minerals are lost in this process.

Immune System: A complex system of organs and substances that protect the dog's body against disease and infection.

International Unit (IU): A unit of measurement that signifies biological activity for the fat soluble vitamins A, D, and E.

Jaundice: A yellowing of the skin due to the appearance of bile in the blood, indicating liver disease.

Keratin: A form of protein found in hair, skin, and feathers.

Lactose: The sugar in milk made up of glucose and galactose. A carbohydrate present only in the milk of mammals. Aids in absorption of calcium and phosphorus. Adults may have difficulty digesting lactose.

Lecithin: A colourless compound found in brain, nerves, egg yolk and soybean. Is a combination of fatty acids and is an important source of choline and inositol. Used to metabolizes fats, and treatment of skin disorders.

Malt: Usually barley grain that has been steeped in water, germinated and dried.

Megadose: A large intake of a nutrient.

Nutrient: A substance in food providing energy, helping in the regulation of metabolism, or building, maintaining or repairing tissues.

Nutrition: The process by which animals and plants take in and utilize food material. Also the study of the nourishment of humans, animals or plants.

Obese: Overweight, obesity: body fat weight more than 20% above ideal body weight.

Organic: A substance that contains carbon.

Oxidation: The combining with oxygen. Spoilage and rancidity of carbohydrates and fats. Prevented by antioxidants or hydrogenation.

Pasteurization: A process in which a food is heated for a determined time to destroy pathogenic organisms. Also lessening the nutrient values of proteins, vitamins, minerals and enzymes.

Pad: Sole of the foot.

Pancreas: An organ within the abdomen that produces and secretes various digestive enzymes and the hormone insulin.

Photosynthesis: The process whereby plants, utilizing the sun's energy, manufacture carbohydrates in their chlorophyll-containing tissues.

Phytate: A substance in unleavened whole grains that binds to minerals in the dog's intestines and inhibits their absorption.

Pica: The practice of eating non-food items; feces, dirt, wood.

Preservatives: Chemical substances added to foods to protect against spoilage, discoloration, and decay by destroying or inhibiting the growth of microorganisms.

Quiet eye: A non-inflamed eye.

RDA's: Recommended Dietary Allowances are guidelines for humans to the quantities of nutrients that should be eaten every day.

Rectum: Last portion of large intestine extending to the anus.

Refined: The process in which the coarse parts are removed; for example, the refining of whole wheat removes the bran and the germ leaving the endosperm or white flour.

Rendering: Process were fat is separate from livestock carcasses.

Requirement: The amount of a nutrient needed by the dog to prevent deficiency symptoms.

Respiratory Tract: The lungs and their airways.

Retinol: Vitamin A

Retinol Equivalents (RE): A unit of measurement for vitamin A; 1 RE = 1 mcg or 3.33 IU of vitamin A as retinol.

Riboflavin: Vitamin B_2

Rickets: Abnormal bone development due to a lack of vitamin D.

Salt: Common salt, or sodium chloride.

Sebum: An oily secretion from the sebaceous glands of the skin.

Sweetbread: Packing house term for pancreas.

Tannin: Tannic acid. A yellowish, astringent compound in tea.

Tocopherol: Vitamin E.

Toxicity: The ability of being poisonous.

Trace Mineral: Minerals required by the dog in very low amounts.

Tripe: Packing house term for the rumens of cattle and sheep.

Ulcer: Damage to the outside layer of the skin or the lining of the stomach appearing as an erosion with inflammation and pain.

Vegan: A strict vegetarian who eats no food of animal origin.

Variable formula: A commercial pet food formula in which a number of ingredients are listed. Those used will depend on availability, cost and will change between batches.

Whelping: The act of giving birth for the dog.

Whey: The watery part of milk left after the protein-rich curd (casein) is separated in the process of making cheese. Rich in lactose and lactalbumin, some fats and minerals.

Whole Grain: An unrefined grain that retains its edible outside layers (bran) and its highly nutritious inner germ.

Xerophthalmia: A condition of the eye producing a dry and lusterless eyeball, due to a deficiency of vitamin A.

Yeast: The common name of the fungi, Saccharomyces, used for leavening bread and producing alcoholic fermentation. Brewer's yeast is yeast obtained as a by-product in the brewing of beer.

Zinc: A blue-white metal, required by the dog in minute amounts but toxic in high levels.

Zoonosis: Diseases of animals that may be transmitted to man.

INDEX

Good Food for Your Dog by Jean Powell, Citadel Press, Secaucus, New Jersey, 1981

Bones To Biscuits, The Dog Foodbook by Linda McDonald, Oakland Press, Inc. 283 South Lake Avenue, Pasadena, California, 1977

The Healthy Cat and Dog Cook Book by Joan Harper, Pet Press, Richland Center, Wisconsin 53581, 1988

Nutrition and Your Dog by Josephine Banks and Paul Loeb, Pocket Books a division of Simon and Schuster Inc. New York, 1989

The Complete Herbal Handbook for the Dog and Cat by Juliette de Bairacli Levy, Arco Publishing, Inc. New York, 1986

Natural Health for Dogs and Cats by Richard H. Pitcairn DVM, Ph.D. and Susan Hubble Pitcarian, Rodale Press, Emmaus, Pa. 1982

The Collins Guide to Dog Nutrition by Donald R. Collins DVM, Howell Book House Inc. New York, 1987

Every Dog, the Complete Book of Dog Care by Eric Allan and Rowan Blogg, Oxford University Press, Melbourne, 1992

The Dog Lover's Cookbook by Bernard Tonken DVM, The Main Street Press, Pittstown, New Jersey

Successful Kennel Management by Mark Taynton & Shelia T. Slik, CEPCO Business Systems, Inc. Tallahassee, Florida

How To Have A Healthier Dog, The Benefits of Vitamins and Minerals for Your Dog's Life Cycles by Wendell O. Belfield DVM and Martin Zucker, Doubleday & Company, Inc. Garden City, New York

Basic Guide to Canine Nutrition, Gaines Professional Services, 250 North Street, White Plains, N. Y. 10625

Caring for Your Older Dog by Kathleen Berman and Bill Landesman, Arco Publishing, Inc. New York, 1984

The Labrador Retriever by Dorothy Howe, T.F.H. Publications, Inc. Ltd. 211 West Sylvania Ave. Neptune City, NJ 07753

Pet Care, by A.T.B. Edney and I.B. Hughes, Blackwell/Year Book Medical Publishers, Inc.

The Doggie Biscuit Book, by Moneca Litton, General Communications Corporation Ltd. North Vancouver, B.C.

Holistic Animal News, PO Box 9384, Seattle, WA, 98109

A Commonsense Guide to Feeding Your Dog and Cat, CVMA Pet Food Certification Program 339 Booth St. Ottawa, Ont. K1R 7K1

How to Order Additional Books and Prints

Our Pet's INC.

Our Pet's Inc.
P.O. Box 2094,
Fort Macleod, Alberta,
Canada TOL OZO

Let's Cook For Our Dog $ **19.95** each
(Shipping, handling and GST included)

Please send _____ **Books @ 19.95** each

(Watch for **Let's Cook for Our Cat** in 1994)

Watercolour Prints @ $ **24.95** each
(Shipping, handling and GST included)

Watercolour prints are 11"/17" on 100# stock
Prints will be shipped in cardboard envelope
Prints will be signed and dated by the artist

Print   number ordered

1. **Bath Time** .... _____
2. **Who Left The Gate Open?** .... _____
3. **Let's Play** .... _____
4. **Black Lab** .... _____
5. **Cocker Spaniel** .... _____
6. **German Shepherd** .... _____
7. **Puppy** .... _____
8. **Schnauzer** .... _____

Total prints .... _____

Prints _____ @ $ **24.95** = _____

Books plus Prints = _____

Make cheque or money order payable to:

Our Pet's Inc.
P.O. Box 2094
Fort Macleod, Alberta
TOL OZO

Orders outside of Canada: paid in U.S. funds by cheque or money order drawn on a Canadian or U.S. bank. (Shipping included)

Allow several weeks for delivery.

Thank You

I would like to order Our Pet's Books and Watercolour prints listed on the reverse side.

NAME _____
   (please print)
Street/P.O. Box _____

City/town _____

Province/State _____ **Postal code/Zip**_____

Gift Giving

I would like to send **Let's Cook For Our Dog** and **Watercolour prints** to the following person.

Let's Cook For Our Dog _____ @ 19.95 .... $ _____

Watercolour Prints _____ @ 24.95 .... $ _____

   (signed and dated by the artist)

   Bath Time _____, Who Left The Gate Open _____,

   Let's Play _____, Black Lab. _____,

   Cocker Spaniel _____, German Shepherd _____,

   Puppy _____, Schnauzer _____

      Total books and prints.............................. $ _____

   (Shipping, handling and GST included)

A Gift For You

NAME _____
   (please print)
Street/P.O. Box _____

City/town _____

Province/State _____ **Postal code/Zip**_____

From

_____
Gift card message

_____

_____

_____

How to Order Additional Books and Prints

Our Pet's INC.

Our Pet's Inc.
P.O. Box 2094,
Fort Macleod, Alberta,
Canada TOL OZO

Let's Cook For Our Dog $ 19.95 each
(Shipping, handling and GST included)

Please send _____ **Books @ 19.95** each

(Watch for **Let's Cook for Our Cat** in 1994)

Watercolour Prints @ **$ 24.95** each
(Shipping, handling and GST included)

Watercolour prints are 11"/17" on 100# stock
Prints will be shipped in cardboard envelope
Prints will be signed and dated by the artist

Print   number ordered

1. **Bath Time** .... _____
2. **Who Left The Gate Open?** .... _____
3. **Let's Play** .... _____
4. **Black Lab** .... _____
5. **Cocker Spaniel** .... _____
6. **German Shepherd** .... _____
7. **Puppy** .... _____
8. **Schnauzer** .... _____

Total prints .... _____

Prints _____ @ **$ 24.95** = _____

Books plus Prints = _____

Make cheque or money order payable to:

Our Pet's Inc.
P.O. Box 2094
Fort Macleod, Alberta
TOL OZO

Orders outside of Canada: paid in U.S. funds by cheque or money order drawn on a Canadian or U.S. bank. (Shipping included)

Allow several weeks for delivery.

Thank You

I would like to order Our Pet's Books and Watercolour prints listed on the reverse side.

NAME _____
   (please print)
Street/P.O. Box _____

City/town _____

Province/State _____ **Postal code/Zip** _____

Gift Giving

I would like to send **Let's Cook For Our Dog** and **Watercolour prints** to the following person.

Let's Cook For Our Dog _____ @ **19.95** .... $ _____

Watercolour Prints _____ @ **24.95** .... $ _____

   (signed and dated by the artist)

   Bath Time _____, Who Left The Gate Open _____,

   Let's Play _____, Black Lab. _____,

   Cocker Spaniel _____, German Shepherd _____,

   Puppy _____, Schnauzer _____

      Total books and prints .... $ _____

   (Shipping, handling and GST included)

A Gift For You

NAME _____
   (please print)
Street/P.O. Box _____

City/town _____

Province/State _____ **Postal code/Zip** _____

From

_____
Gift card message

_____

_____

_____

SUGGESTIONS AND COMMENTS

We Would Like To Hear From You

If you have any comments about the book and how we can make it better please write to the publisher, Our Pet's Inc. at the address below.

If you have a favorite recipe that you have been using and would like to share it, we would be glad to hear from you and perhaps include it in future printings. If we should use your recipe full credits will be given and a free copy of the new printing will be sent to you in appreciation. Thank you.

Our Pet's Inc. P.O. 2094, Fort Macleod, Alberta, Canada TOL OZO

COMMENTS

_____

_____

_____

_____

_____

_____

_____

_____

_____

_____

Name _____

Street/P.O. Box _____

City/town _____

Province/State_____Postal code/Zip _____

Pet's name_____Breed_____Age____Sex _____

Pet's food: Brands _____

Where purchased? _____

Amount fed/day_____Table scraps, yes____no _____

Pet's favorite recipe _____

_____

_____

_____

_____

AUTHOR PROFILE

Dr. Edmund R. Dorosz has been a practicing veterinarian and college instructor to Animal Health Technicians for many years. After receiving his Bachelors of Science in Agriculture (B.S.A.) in 1966 and his Doctor of Veterinary Medicine (D.V.M) in 1971, he was engaged in veterinary practice as well as instructing Animal Health Technicians.

In his many years of dealing with animal health and animal feeding, nutrition was an important component. Always attempting to be practical with animal owners and their animals, he strived to educate his clients and students to look at the big picture. He asked them to understand and always question what they were doing with respect to the welfare of their animals.

Seeing the need for a practical approach to pet nutrition and feeding in our changing world inspired the books Let's Cook For Our Dog and Let's Cook For Our Cat.

He has always had an interest in art, drawing and painting, since childhood. The illustrations and watercolour paintings in the books are some of his latest works.